From Bihar to Tihar

From Bihar
to Tihar

Kanhaiya Kumar

Translated by Vandana R. Singh

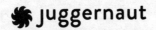

JUGGERNAUT BOOKS
KS House, 118 Shahpur Jat, New Delhi 110049, India

First published by Juggernaut Books 2016

ISBN 978-81-9323-727-4

Typeset in Adobe Caslon Pro by R. Ajith Kumar, New Delhi

Printed and bound at Thomson Press India Ltd

Dedicated to the toiling masses

Everyone has his or her own story but one person's life is often another person's fiction. If you are to understand me, then you must enter my world, see things the way I see them.

I welcome you to accompany me in the political journey of an ordinary student from an ordinary village of this 'not so ordinary' country.

Contents

Prologue

It was my fifteenth day in Tihar. The Delhi High Court had granted me bail the previous day, but I had to stay in prison for another day because of unfinished paperwork.

After lunch, a constable came to my cell. Despite the security provisions, some constables in the jail did manage to slip through the restrictions and talk to me.

'This is your last day. Today you'll be released.'

I got up from the bed and walked to the door of the cell.

He said, 'I've come to you with a question. But first I'll tell you a story.'

The story went something like this...

Once upon a time there was a king. The king loved his people and was very popular. The people loved their king, the kingdom was very prosperous and everyone was happy. The king had one daughter. But he was now getting old and was beginning to worry about his kingdom, his people, their well-being, his successor – he had a lot to think about.

Who would rule after him and who would marry his daughter? He wanted to find an answer to both these questions. He decided to look for a clever groom for his daughter so that he would take care of her as well as of the kingdom. He considered many princes, met them and talked to them but didn't find any of them suitable.

One day, one of his courtiers suggested holding a competition. 'You get your daughter married to the winner and also hand over the kingdom to him. After that you can rest in peace.'

The king liked this suggestion. All the neighbouring kingdoms were informed that a competition had been organized to find a suitable match for the princess and a successor to the king. There was a waterfall up in the hills flowing down to a lake which was infested with crocodiles. The competition involved jumping into the lake from the falls and coming out safely.

Princes from all castes and religions came from far and wide for the competition. It was a golden opportunity. All the participants lined up and walked up to the waterfall one by one. But on reaching the spot and looking down from the great height of the falls, they became terrified. The knowledge that the lake was full of crocodiles added to their fear.

One after another, all suitors refused. Only one man had

the courage to jump, and he succeeded in swimming out of the lake and reaching the designated place. Ecstatic, the king got his daughter married to him and gave him his entire kingdom to rule. Soon after, the old man went away into the forest.

As soon as the old king left, the new one had a huge throne built. It was so high that he needed to climb several steps every day to sit on it.

'So Kanhaiya, the question is, if a man such as this one put his life in danger and won the competition with his intelligence and quick thinking, why did he do something so irrational as soon as he became king?'

Part 1

Childhood

1

'What is your name?' he asked.

'Kanhaiya Kumar.'

There was a wooden table between us; he was sitting across me on the other side.

'Father's name?'

'Jai Shankar Singh.'

'Mother's name?'

'Meena Devi.'

There were only two other people in the room with me in the Lodhi Road thana. But the short, sharp questions of my interrogator in khaki uniform made me feel trapped and claustrophobic, as if I was in a crowded cell with no room to breathe.

'What's the name of your village?'

'Masnadpur, Bihat.'

'How many brothers are you?'

'Three. One older than me, one younger.'

7

A third person entered the room. Walking in, he rapped me on the head and made me stand up. 'How come you sat down? Chalo, get up, *deshdrohi saale!*'

'How many sisters? Married?' The other man continued with his questions. I answered as calmly as possible, focusing on his nameplate so I could memorize his name.

'Only one sister. She's married.'

He took out my confiscated phone and dialled a number. I couldn't tell who he was speaking to but could hear that he was asking a few questions. Then he told the voice on the other end that his son had been arrested.

It was my father. Suddenly it was as though the cramped room I was in was filled with my family – my mother, my village and my people, all of whom had seemed far away only a few hours ago. I started to worry about my father, who has a heart condition, and the terrible effect this news could have on him. I thought of my mother, with whom I had not spoken in many months. I thought of my village, which was bound to be affected by the news that one of their boys had been sent to prison.

JNU, my studies, my friends, student politics – these were what formed my daily world and occupied my thoughts. But the cops' questions had forced me to think about the past that had shaped my present, my village, my parents, my siblings. And as it became clearer and clearer to me that I had not just been brought in for a conversation with the thana cops, that I was in fact about to be arrested, it was the faces from my childhood that returned to me most vividly.

2

My village, Bihat, is connected to the world through the Patna–Begusarai railway line – somewhere in between the Mokama and Barauni stations. Surrounded by the Barauni Thermal Power Station, Fertilizer Corporation of India and Barauni Refinery, this biggish village of 67,000 people has produced several politicians, ministers, judges, governors, administrators, police officers, athletes, poets, artists and actors.

A distant relative of mine, Ramcharitra Singh, the first minister for power and irrigation in Bihar, came from this village. He is credited with the development of this area and setting up a string of factories here. His son, Comrade Chandrashekhar Singh, developed communism in this area and was responsible for strengthening its base. He too went on to become the power and irrigation minister of the state in the Karpoori Thakur government.

Bihat was the most prosperous of all villages in

Begusarai. Each ward (the administrative unit of a village) here had a primary school, and every panchayat had a primary health care clinic, five middle schools and two high schools. The communist party had a strong presence in Bihar until 1996 with the result that women here participated in public life far more than they did in other areas. But it did not mean that everyone in the village was prosperous. Huge inequalities still existed in Bihat.

I was born in the Masnadpur locality of this village.

There was nothing unusual about my birth. My life was a repeat of the lives of all children born in poor families in India's villages – they are given a name, they start to read and write, and then they grow up, some continuing school, many dropping out to work. There are just a few variations.

My family was very poor. Previously I would introduce myself by my father's name. But now I think children should tell their mother's name first. My mother, Meena Devi, is more educated than my father and was the main breadwinner of our family for many years. My father, Jai Shankar Singh, didn't take the class ten exams but my mother had passed them.

Pitaji was a farmer by profession but he farmed only occasionally as he didn't have much land to farm and he often worked as a daily labourer to feed us all. When he developed a host of health complications, Ma managed to get a job. Under the Sarv Shiksha Abhiyan, government crèches called anganwadis had been opened all over the country to educate and take care of children up to five years of age. It was in one of these centres in our village that Ma got the job of a helper at three thousand rupees a month.

I have a sister, Juhi, and two brothers – Manikant is older than me and Prince is younger. As a child I didn't know my caste, perhaps because at that age it was not important. But today this is a critical issue in India. So it is crucial to share that – but for an accident of birth – I belong to the general category and this is part of my social identity over which I have no control. I don't believe in religion either, but in this country even non-believers are viewed as belonging to a religion and no one really has any option but to accept that. You are born with your religion, you don't choose it – and my family happen to be Hindu.

Nanaji, my maternal grandfather, used to be an active Congress party worker – complete with the Congress cap, etc. It doesn't seem appropriate to call it the 'Gandhi topi' because Gandhi never wore a cap. Dadaji, my paternal grandfather, was a supporter of the Communist Party of India (CPI), though he was not a member or a card holder. He worked as head foreman at the Barauni Thermal Power Station. He was also a member of the All India Trade Union Congress (AITUC), the country's first labour organization. This was how his connection with the communist party began. The economic condition determines the political affiliation.

Pitaji's political leanings were somewhat at a tangent with the rest of the family's. I'm not sure if this was a form of rebellion against the family or his own self, but while the entire family supported and voted for the CPI, Pitaji sympathized with a CPI breakaway group, CPI (Marxist-Leninist) Liberation, which believed that revolution could be brought about only at gunpoint.

He eventually gave up his militant views – perhaps acknowledging the faltering nature of the movement or the family's own need for him – and settled down to domesticity. From an unstable life where he was barely earning any income, he dedicated himself to providing for his children, taking care of the family and occasionally travelling for work, something he loved to do. But his faith in democracy was never weakened and he always went out to vote. I suspect he voted for the CPI.

My family's political background is not of the family's alone, but holds good for tens of thousands in this country. Large parts of India had originally been followers of the Congress party. My family and village too had Congress leanings in the past. Nanaji was one example but of course the most prominent Congress leader from our village was the minister Ramcharitra Singh, our distant relative. But his son, Chandrashekhar Singh, went to Banaras Hindu University (BHU) for higher studies and there, under the influence of revolutionaries, abandoned the Congress.

The son's political journey became the political journey of our village. Chandrashekhar Singh came back home inflamed by Marxist ideology. Under his influence, much of the youth in the village joined the CPI. Congress influence started to weaken. The Congress party had never fulfilled the expectations raised at the time of Independence. We were still poor, opportunities were scarce, inequality was vast. And so the youth, educated class, labourers, farmers, Dalits and the poor moved towards the more leftist party. It didn't take long for a significant footprint to be established.

As a fallout of this, Ramcharitra Singh had to resign from the cabinet. He had come into the limelight for being a minister in the Congress government whose son had become a communist leader.

At that time, the so-called Hindu nationalists of today were not to be seen. The hooligans and rowdies of the Congress would later become Bharatiya Janata Party (BJP) people. But the village traditionally used to have Congress people, communists and socialists.

3

Despite the influence of the communist party in my village and my family, patriarchy, casteism and religiosity continued to exist. In my childhood I saw the paradoxical coexistence of progressiveness, modernity and orthodox thinking in my family.

On the one hand, Dadaji wanted my mother – his daughter-in-law, whose studies had been discontinued by her father – to continue studying after marriage. On the other hand, even though he was a non-believer, he made all the Chhath puja arrangements for Dadi and accompanied her to the ghat carrying a large basket in which all the items required for the puja were carefully arranged. I'm not sure whether this was religious devotion or love for his wife. So I grew up seeing a mix of modernity and rustic culture in my family.

Pitaji was never interested in the books prescribed in the syllabus but he read a lot from outside it. And even though he did not hold a degree, he was very knowledgeable and had a sound understanding of issues. However, in our country a degree is considered more valuable than either knowledge or understanding. And in this Ma overtook Pitaji.

In Ma, one can see the problems faced by all rural women but also get a sense of how exceptional she was. She was married while still a girl, soon to become a mother who had family responsibilities, but nevertheless she continued her schooling. It is said that women are hard-working and never complain about anything; the reality is that the social structure forces them to become so. Ma was no different, and she managed all these roles wonderfully. She brought up her children, took care of her in-laws and steadily pursued her education. This is why she has always been more important to me than my father.

The only other family member I admire as much is Dadaji, who used to walk a distance of thirty-five kilometres from the village each day for his studies.

When Ramcharitra Singh, who was Dadaji's chacha, was appointed minister, many factories were set up in Begusarai. Dadaji found a job as a helper in one of them and later rose to be head foreman.

This brought about an improvement in the family's financial situation. Dadaji educated his daughters and they eventually became teachers and got married into educated families. Because of Dadaji's hard work, our family slowly began to climb its way up from poverty. In fact, most of my extended family – my chacha, my bua, etc. – were much better off than us. However, Pitaji, consumed by the fervour of revolutionary politics, could not devote much time to earning a livelihood.

Pitaji tended to mingle more with castes other than his own. He adopted their ideas and social habits. At that time a protest against caste-based exploitation was building up in the village. While our entire family had faith in democracy and the parliamentary system, Pitaji rubbished all this as an eyewash and believed that such a system could never end exploitation. If a zamindar was being oppressive, he had to be taught a lesson and killed. And so while his siblings and cousins were studying and diligently building their careers, Pitaji stayed away from home, living his own dreams of revolution. But living one's dreams is not so easy.

Pitaji's political engagement had a big impact on me, my siblings and Ma. Our financial situation became steadily worse over the years even as the rest of our relatives began to prosper. Being poor is a curse like no other – it is a crime to be poor and the pain of poverty is unique in its ability to hurt.

To be able to understand exploitation, one must be the exploited; for the privileged, the stories of exploitation are just a fairy tale.

4

My childhood seemed full of small mysteries. These may not have amounted to much for adults, but to my younger self, my origins seemed strange, even shrouded. For instance, I called Ma 'Didi'. Perhaps I picked this up from Mama, my maternal uncle, who had accompanied Ma to her new home when she got married and had lived with her ever since. Only when I was in class eight or maybe class nine did I realize that one's mother was not addressed as 'didi'.

Because of our financial difficulties, my older brother and sister lived away from us with my two aunts, and so we siblings didn't really grow up together. I was in class eight when one of my aunts died and my sister came back to live with us. Though I knew she was my sister, she felt like a stranger.

Now I had to learn to share space with her, and we would often quarrel over where to keep our books and combs, etc. A casualty of meagre means is that it leaves the siblings' relations malnourished. But I accepted her as my sister and made her a part of my life. I never called her Didi, though; I called her by her name instead. One day when my friends began pulling my leg about this, I started addressing my mother as 'Ma' and my sister as 'Didi'.

Then there was the mystery of my name. My brother was born on Janmashtami, Lord Krishna's birthday, and he was named Manikant. No one remembered the day of my birth but my name was Kanhaiya, which is another name for Lord Krishna. I often used to wonder why this was so. If anything my brother had a better claim to the name Kanhaiya. Later when I went to school, children talked about where they had been born, which place or hospital they had been born in. I had no such story to tell. One day on returning from school, I asked Ma about my birth.

She said that on the morning of my birth she was cooking like she did every day. She had walked over to the corner of the room where the atta was kept in a sack when she felt a sharp pain and went into labour. I was born next to that sack. I have often since looked at that corner and thought to myself, so this was my hospital.

The mystery of my name also unravelled eventually. I may be thin now but I'm told I wasn't always like this. I was born a big, heavy baby, and gave Ma a lot of trouble during labour. Because of Pitaji's uncertain life, Dadaji and Dadiji had decided to move in with their pregnant daughter-in-law. The arrangement was that they would spend their salary and pension on Ma and us children, and Ma would take care of them.

So Ma was well looked after during her pregnancy and I was born very healthy. Soon after my birth, the women from the neighbourhood visited us and when my chachi held me, a fat, dimpled little infant, in her lap she said I looked just like Kanhaiya, a term of endearment for Lord Krishna.

And so I was named Kanhaiya. No horoscope was made for me, no one studied the stars under which I was born and no pandit was consulted to find out what the first letter of my name should be. It would be several years before I'd come to know my actual date of birth.

In all the confusion, no one remembered the date of the event and so when it was time to take admission in school the teacher randomly wrote 2 January as my birthday. Even today this is my date of birth on record. But my teacher and I knew it wasn't the right date, of course, because this is the common practice in rural areas. I always remained curious to know the truth. I discovered it by chance only after my class ten examinations.

We were short of notebooks and paper to write on so

I would use Pitaji's old diaries while studying. One day, I saw the following entry: 'Today a guest has come to my home.' The page was dated 27 March. The year was the same as that of my birth. I asked Ma and she said, 'This is the date of your birth. Your father had written this down.'

And so at fifteen, I came to know when I had been born.

5

I don't clearly remember when I started going to school. All I know is that I initially used to go with my chachi and later with Ma. The school's name was Madhya Vidyalaya, Masnadpur. It was a fun place – a small school set up before Independence. It had only two rooms but they were spacious. When I started, there were twelve teachers but by the time I left only two remained.

Like all small village schools, this one too had very few facilities. If a child had to use the toilet he was not allowed to ask directly. He had to say, 'Madam, can I take five minutes off?' Those five minutes for 'using the toilet' were spent in the open air of the fields because the school had no toilet. Nor did it have a library. We didn't even have a pole to put up the national flag and a few bricks were hastily piled up together when it was to be hoisted.

Talking of flags, 15 August and 26 January were the most fun days at school because we were then given something to eat. Of course, the treat depended on the teacher. If the teacher was generous enough we got delicious jalebis but if we were unlucky to have a miserly one we had to be satisfied with cheap, locally made chocolates.

As I grew older I became physically weak and couldn't take part in games or athletics. I started taking an interest in singing, writing, public speaking and sketching and, because of this, these two days became even more important in my life. The students who participated in activities were given larger portions of chocolate and this meant I celebrated our nation's milestones with extra zeal.

Like all children, I was also very naughty and created mischief all over the village with a group of boys. We were daring but would make sure we never got caught. Once we had no money to buy firecrackers so I lit the *sarpat* grass (used to thatch roofs), which popped just like the crackers do. We were enjoying the crackle when the fire started spreading and reached a neighbour's cattle shed, which had a cow in it. We ran away in terror. Luckily the fire was brought under control but not before our actions had created a real furore.

In the summer we would go to the orchards and steal all the ripe mangoes and when the owners shook the trees to get their yield they would only get raw ones. The same happened with jackfruit. We would also play-act police and thieves and run riot in the paddy fields. Complaints of these pranks would reach home, but thankfully Pitaji and my uncle never pursued these charges.

At school too I was no different. The children sitting in front of the class studied and those at the back fought with each other while the teacher usually dozed off. I, meanwhile, would be busy making paper planes and flying them or stealing chalk from the classroom. We also liked fighting with each other and copying the fight scenes in the films we had watched the previous day on the television.

I usually stood first in class but then everyone passed anyway. They say your own happiness doesn't please you – it is other people's unhappiness that makes you happy. But in my school, no one had these problems because even those who were mischievous, who fought with the other kids or never came to school moved up to the next class.

The teaching was of mixed quality. The teachers who were keen on imparting knowledge taught us well. But there were as many, if not more, teachers who never paid attention to us, who went through their day without showing any interest in the lessons, and some who used to tell us to just write our names on answer sheets and then they passed us. Government schools are in bad condition because people want to sit in Parliament and government offices but are hesitant to get their children taught in government schools.

Despite all these shortcomings, we did learn something. Learning counting and about science, social norms, the nation, patriotism, all this came from school.

6

It was December and my exam results were expected. Normally, I never waited for them and would take the next year's books from a senior and start reading them, especially the Hindi poetry. The syllabus was not much more challenging than this. Even in class six, no one knew anything beyond the twenty-six letters of English.

As I walked towards the school, some children returning from there told me I had stood first. I turned back and headed home. On the way I met Kaviji, our village poet, reading the newspaper. Seeing me he said, 'So, young man, where are you coming from?'

'Just returning after hearing the result.'

'What is it then?'

'Stood first again, what else?'

I was to realize much later how arrogant my reply was – at that time I was intoxicated by my performance. Kaviji looked at me and asked, 'Achha, you stood first?

Now tell me how much is *unhattar* [sixty-nine]?'

'Seven and nine,' I replied confidently.

'Very good? And *unyaasi* [seventy-nine]?'

'Eight and nine.'

He chuckled and said, 'You certainly deserve to stand first.'

Full of myself, I returned home, my vanity even more inflated by this praise from our educated local poet. But that night his words rang differently in my mind. Had there been a note of laughter in his voice when he complimented me?

I started to think of what he had asked me and opened my maths book to make sure my answers were right. That was when I realized I didn't even know counting and I had topped my class in spite of this. It was a pathetic state of affairs – this much I understood even then, but that this was the result of the pathetic state of affairs of the education system, society and the country I came to know only later.

I decided then that I had to read beyond whatever was being taught in school. Staying awake at night, I started studying maths, science and social science by the light of a diya – there was no saying for how long the electricity supply would be available. People began citing me as an example to their children, commenting on how I stayed awake reading late into the night with only a diya.

My parents could do little to help me in this ambition. But my principal at school, Urvashiji, started putting pressure on Pitaji saying that he needed to bring in some stable income for the sake of my future. 'This child works very hard; you need to think about your own work now,' she told him.

Shortly thereafter, Pitaji drew back from his politics and began to focus on his family and my education. Urvashiji's words had come at a time when he was disillusioned by the movement – the party had changed track and moved from the gun to the ballot paper. Perhaps it was both these factors that led him to make such a monumental shift.

He had never kept any cattle at home because he didn't want his children to get caught up looking after them. He decided to give up smoking. The milk that was bought for making tea was discontinued. Savings from both these things went towards paying for my tuition lessons.

The family had to make do with black tea. In cities, people might drink black tea as a sign of refinement, but in the village people like their milky tea. My brother Prince, especially, loved his tea, often finishing off what was left in Ma's cup. He was extremely upset that he was being deprived of milk tea for the sake of my schooling.

My first tutor was Parmanand Yadav. He was a generous figure in my life, a man who taught me how to read in English and much else. He worked himself to the bone teaching for twelve to thirteen hours each day and travelling the entire locality to reach his students. Some of the kids he taught were from homes with a car, TV and telephone but these were just a handful. Most didn't have such luxuries. Of all his students I was the worst off.

At the end of every month he gave all his students a test, and I started to top each one. This only added to Pitaji's problems. Another name now joined the list of people putting pressure on him about my future. Urvashiji had insisted I needed tuition to reach my full promise. Parmanandji went one step further, suggesting I be taken out of the government school and put into a private school.

Our education system had undergone a long period of transition starting from 1986, when a new education policy was introduced by the Rajiv Gandhi government. This had sown the first seeds of privatization in the sector.

Earlier, a state primarily had government schools and children from different economic backgrounds studied in the same school. But it wasn't as though all government schools were about social equality. Those from poorer homes studied in middle and high schools run by the state government while those from more prosperous backgrounds went to Kendriya Vidyalayas and also took extra tuition. Children of government employees tended to get admission to these schools and sometimes children from their extended families were passed off as their own and given admission there.

In 1985, a new, even more elite set of government schools called Jawahar Navodaya Vidyalayas were introduced. This was a highly competitive kind of school and very hard to get into. Ten years on, we had begun to see the growth of private schools. So this was the new terrain my family had to find its way through in 1996.

Parmanandji told Pitaji that he should send me to a private school and that he would simultaneously prepare me for the Jawahar Navodaya Vidyalaya.

Pitaji decided to follow my tutor's advice. He got me admitted to a private school called Sunrise Public School and bought an enormous, heavy workbook to help me prepare to get into the Jawahar Navodaya Vidyalaya.

My monthly school fees were forty rupees a month and Parmanandji's fees were twenty-five rupees. The school was three kilometres away and money was arranged for the school rickshaw, an additional sixty rupees. This was a big burden on my family since my parents earned only twenty-five hundred rupees a month.

New shoes, new clothes and new notebooks for different subjects were bought for my new school. I was excited and showed off my shoes to everyone. My happiness fuelled my brother's resentment. Thank God he didn't rip apart the shoes in his jealousy. We were almost the same age and I had new shoes while he didn't even have a hawai chappal.

But I had no understanding of this inequality then. I was simply enjoying my sudden riches. Today, happiness is dependent on not just what you have but also on how many people don't have it. The more you are able to show off your prosperity, the more content you are.

7

Sunrise Public School opened up new social layers. When I was studying at the government school, I didn't understand class distinctions. There was no uniform there and everyone wore their own clothes to school. In the private school there was a prescribed uniform. When people say the uniform camouflages social class they've got it all wrong. Actually it's the uniform that gives away class.

No matter what children wear to school, by the end of the day their clothes are dirty. Only those who have several sets can be in clean clothes every day. I had only one set of the uniform. By Friday it was filthy and sometimes actually stinking. Ma didn't realize this. In our family I was the first to go to a private school so none of us knew the dos and don'ts.

In the government school the books were in Hindi. Ma in those days taught me every day while she cooked meals.

But in the new school she couldn't do this. There was a school diary, homework, classwork, separate notebooks, etc., and other than Hindi and Sanskrit all these books were in English.

This created an unpleasant distancing in the mother–son relationship. I started telling Ma things like 'What do you know? You don't know anything. You've only studied in a government school, I'm in a private school' and so on. I also became aggressive towards my brothers and started showing off my knowledge of English. Ma never punished me, Pitaji was rarely home, and the entire neighbourhood looked up to me. I became very arrogant.

But while I could boss over Ma and bully the kids of my area, I couldn't lord over the children at my school. The class divide there left me isolated. Most of the kids had nice clothes and shoes, and several pairs of socks. They all looked clean. Most of them wore trousers, locally referred to as 'full pant'. Poor kids like me wore shorts, that is, 'half pant', to school, because we could get two half pants from the fabric needed for one full pant. It was in class ten that I wore full pants for the first time in my life, as part of the uniform given out by the government high school.

Each day, there was something or the other in the private school that separated me from the others. Very young children wore mufflers, which were quite expensive. Only those who could afford them or had someone who could knit one for them used mufflers. Ma knitted a cap for me and when I wore it to school for the first time the other children took it off and began playing with it, tossing it up in the air like a ball. I felt thoroughly ashamed and regretted the fact that from being at the top of the pile in the government school I had been reduced to a nonentity here.

For the first time I was face-to-face with all the hardships that is the lot of students from the weaker sections. The children in my private school didn't just wear good clothes, they also had cars and motorcycles to commute. It was a different world altogether. Until now I hadn't even been really familiar with my entire village; my knowledge was limited to my locality. But now I began to learn about the whole area. I started sensing the difference between children living in kuchcha houses and pukka houses. I started measuring time by the speed of the cars on the road. Difference and discrimination became part of my psyche.

Those early days set the tone of my future. I was already embarrassed about how poor my family was. Soon I began to lose my confidence about the one thing I had always been sure of – my studies. In my second day at the new school, I was slapped for the first time in life. The English teacher had asked me to stand up and read. The lesson was 'The Real Princess'. While reading I got stuck at one point and the teacher slapped me.

The third source of embarrassment was to do with my understanding of the cultural norms at Sunrise. At the old school I would read out poetry and sing, and be among the best to do so. In the fine arts class at the new school, the teacher asked each child to sing a song. To make up for what had happened during the English lesson, I was the first to raise my hand. I started singing a patriotic film song, '*Mera rang de basanti chola, maa ye, rang de basanti chola*'.

The entire class burst into amused laughter.

Madam said, 'What kind of a silly song is this? Go and sit down.'

The next boy sang '*Na kajre ki dhaar, na motiyon ka haar*', a popular song from the film *Mohra*. Madam was very happy, while I was shocked. Till then I had believed that singing popular film songs in school was inappropriate.

It was hard for me to get my bearings. It was fine to sing '*Na kajre ki dhaar, na motiyon ka haar*' in the fine arts class. But it was not fine for boys and girls (who sat in different sections of the class) to talk to each other. In fact, it was something to be made fun of. This mix of orthodox thinking and modernity in my new school was far more complex than the environment in my middle-class rural family and my government school.

It took me more than a year to get over my personal inadequacies. My cap and half pant remained unchanged, but I began to slowly make up by doing well in studies and in literary and cultural activities. But that first year proved to be tough. For the Founding Day celebrations on 12 December, I was not selected for any event – not singing or public speaking.

What really upset me was my academic performance. I went to school to get my result, full of expectation. Half the exhilaration lay in the fact that I carried an empty bag since we didn't have to study on the day of the result. I would usually trudge to school with a heavy bag full of books. The weightless feeling I enjoyed on the big day added to my nervous excitement. But when I heard the result I was totally deflated. I was expecting to be among the top three but for the first time I stood fifth.

I went home with my report card. When I reached home, Ma was washing clothes. That morning on my way to school I had had a little fight with her. I was putting on my uniform without taking a bath and Ma got angry, saying I didn't value the hard work put in by others. I should be clean when I wore my uniform because it took effort and money to keep it clean; even expensive fabric whitener had to be used. We couldn't afford 'aaya *naya Ujala, char boondon wala*', that expensive brand of whitener. We bought loose indigo, which had to be used carefully or it would make clothes blotchy. All this was a great effort for Ma.

The rickshaw puller from school, whom we used to call Bhaiya, called out from a distance, 'Kanhaiyaji, where are you? It's time. We're getting late.' As I was leaving I heard Ma say behind me, 'Walking away unbathed and unwashed...trying to be a dandy...'

My cocky behaviour would pain Ma greatly and our fight that day was especially sore. When I returned with the report card she asked, 'So, what is it?' I have never forgotten her caustic tone, the underlying bitter sarcasm in her question. And as long as I remember this, my feet will stay on the ground – family is the first school and one's mother the first teacher.

Ma was apprehensive that the change in my personality would have an adverse effect on my studies. All said and done, she was a unique woman who was taking care of the family, bringing up her children and, with her face covered under a *ghoonghat*, also going to school herself. She understood the importance of education.

With a heavy heart I said, 'Fifth.'

'You're saying "fifth" as though you've topped the class.'

I had no answer. Ma told me that now I knew where I really stood. 'Earlier you were in a government school where there was hardly any teaching anyway. Now in a private school you've come to know your place,' she told me angrily.

Her words were a big blow to me. The year after, no one scored as high as I did in my class. But I only learnt of it much later. The previous year's result had left such a scar that I didn't go to find out how I'd done, too scared to discover what my rank would be.

Ma didn't ask about that result. In those days Pitaji used to go to Kodarma (then in Bihar, now in Jharkhand) to buy rubble which he then sold in the local market. This kept him away for several days at a stretch. When he returned this time, Pitaji asked about the result. I told him that I hadn't gone to get it. Pitaji borrowed a bike and took me to school. The school was closed but Principal Ramkumarji was in office. Seeing me he said warmly, 'Come, Kanhaiya, come.' His warmth made me even more frightened.

But Pitaji came to my rescue. Steering the conversation in another direction, he said that he hadn't been able to pay the fees for the last few months and so had come now to settle them. The fees were paid and the principal himself wrote out the receipt. Though this was a private school which was trying to ape its urban counterparts, the resources here were limited. In that respect at least, private schools in villages were not that different from government schools – they simply had the word 'convent' or 'public school' in their names.

As we were leaving, Pitaji brought up the real issue. He said he wanted to know my result. Seeing the principal's eyes light up made me go cold all over again. But the principal told him to my relief that I had topped the class.

Even at the December annual celebrations that year, I was ahead of everyone in most events. There was no event in which I did not participate – singing, public speaking, acting, writing, I was everywhere.

One must compare with oneself. There can be no real competition between two different individuals, as their situations and opportunities cannot be similar. The result went a long way in raising my self-esteem. My English too had improved over the year. Parmanandji no longer had the time, and in any case it was difficult for him to help me with the syllabus of Sunrise. So he found another teacher for me. Things were slowly beginning to look good.

8

I hadn't forgotten about the entrance exam for the Jawahar Navodaya Vidyalaya. I filled up the form but discovered I couldn't take the exam. Only those enrolled in a government school were eligible. It was then arranged that I'd study in Sunrise Public School but on paper I'd continue to be a student at my old government school. Urvashiji, the principal, was happy to accommodate me. She wanted me to get selected in the Jawahar Navodaya Vidyalaya as that would make her school look good. Unfortunately, the state government ordered a mass transfer of teachers and Urvashiji had to leave the school. The principal who replaced her was strict and wouldn't bend the rules for me.

This filling-of-forms-and-not-taking-exams was to become a pattern in my life. After class ten I filled the form for the navy and couldn't take the exam. And then years later, the story repeated itself when I filled the

UPSC form and again didn't take the exam. But it was in these periods that my life would take a dramatic turn. I was at the threshold of the first such crossroads.

The Jawahar Vidyalaya dream was over, and it left Pitaji completely broken. He had been nurturing the hope of my admission into such a prestigious government school. Sunrise had always been a stopgap solution; it was simply too expensive for our family. Determined to see me well educated, he began to make inquiries about other schools and started contacting relatives living in the city with whom I could stay while I studied. But nothing worked out. No acquaintance working for the central government agreed to make me their 'son' so I could be eligible for admission in the Kendriya Vidyalaya.

So I continued in Sunrise. As Pitaji's financial situation worsened we had to cut down on various conveniences. After a year my rickshaw was discontinued. The English tuition, which had not just added to my knowledge but also to my self-confidence, was stopped as well. It was becoming clear that I would have to go back to the government school.

In the midst of these tensions, I passed the class seven exam. These years, with their privileges and deprivations, had forced me to grow up. I couldn't see how my actual studies were going to help in my future. I was also beginning to think more deeply about everything I had seen and experienced so far. Caste, religion, patriarchy, rich versus poor – opinions, ideas, questions around these topics played in my mind and began to take shape.

I had begun to feel that a person's merit or ability was unimportant. Given the chance, everyone could sing, act in a play, excel in studies and do well. What mattered was the opportunities you got. I had seen that those who got opportunities moved ahead, and those who didn't got left behind.

I had got some opportunities and so I had done well. But I could also see these opportunities fading, leaving me with no hope. I could see students less capable than me getting admission in elite schools on the basis of their parents' money. Where was the merit in this? It was simply a question of resources.

One of my friends was very good in studies and we were affectionate rivals in school. He had beautiful handwriting and always scored high. But today he fixes punctured tyres in the village. It's not hard to understand why this is so. He, a Dalit boy, was deprived of opportunities. His father, a bus conductor, had died in an accident. After that, my friend had to start working at a cycle repair shop to make ends meet.

In addition, a lot of what we were being taught seemed very irrelevant. For instance, what was the significance of teaching us 'The Real Princess'? It had nothing to do with our lives. In the story there was an arrogant prince who believed that there was no one greater than him.

One night a princess's carriage stops outside his palace, and she asks to spend the night there to break her journey. The prince makes the best possible arrangements for her. Seven mattresses are put on her bed so she can have every comfort. Through the night, the prince checks on her several times, making sure she has everything she needs.

The next morning, the prince asks the princess if she had slept well. The princess replies that she had got a backache as her bedding hadn't been soft enough (a pea had somehow got stuck under the seven mattresses). It then struck the prince that there were other people in this world who were superior to him.

Now what did this story have to do with my life? My life, in which two people could not use the same cup for drinking tea. My life, in which despite being intelligent, you were mocked if you didn't have a muffler and didn't wear full pants, and where you were caned if you stumbled while reading English.

My home didn't have a toilet or a bathroom; we went to the fields to relieve ourselves and bathed at the hand pump. We made do with one light and fan at night to keep our electricity bill down. To iron clothes, Ma used the old kind of press which had to be filled with hot coals. It was a world in which last night's dinner was the morning's breakfast – stale rice or stale roti. Where was this world in our schoolbooks? What was useful was not taught to us and what we were taught was not useful.

These kinds of questions started filling my head. I started looking beyond the syllabus and began to read avidly, especially literature. Premchand became a favourite. Political and cultural activities began to attract me. I started attending workshops conducted by the IPTA – Indian Peoples' Theatre Association – where singing and acting was taught. At the time I would just enjoy myself but the IPTA's activities helped me become the person I am today.

I could see how corruption had ruined the government welfare schemes. The walls of our village carried the words: *Chhath ki cheeni, Diwali ka tel, Bola ho mukhiya kahan gayal?* (Sugar for Chhath, oil for Diwali; tell us, *mukhiya*, where has it all disappeared?) This was a bitter reference to the subsidized rations provided by the government for common people, which never quite reached anyone.

The village head or mukhiya was usually in cahoots with the local dealers. Together they sold subsidized sugar, oil and other goods intended to be given out to ration card holders in the black market. Most villagers got nothing. Only those close to the mukhiya could hope to get a few titbits.

It was around this time that the BJP started gaining ground. In 1996, they had the single largest majority in the general elections, though they couldn't form the government. Neither the Congress nor the CPI could ever match their money power. The BJP's publicity campaigns meant the distribution of mufflers, caps and badges. Party workers drove around distributing pamphlets and flyers, and children loved running after them for fun.

In contrast to this, the CPI took to painting slogans on walls while the Congress simply put up posters. People remained upset with the Congress. At election time the sight of a Congress party worker invariably leads to the chanting of *'Gali gali mein shor hai, Indira Gandhi chor hai'* – implying that it was common knowledge that Indira Gandhi was corrupt. I heard this refrain through my adolescence.

Some scenes stand out from my childhood. It is 1998. I am eleven years old. The United Front government is in power at the centre. The then home minister wants to see Comrade Chandrashekhar's house and decides to take an aerial view of the locked-up property. For the first time a helicopter flies really low over our village, making a loud whirring sound over our roofs. We rush out excitedly to get a glimpse of the aircraft.

Huge rallies were organized in my locality for the general elections that year, and I even took part in some of them. I remember Sushma Swaraj and Shatrughan Sinha coming to our area to campaign for the BJP.

Polling day was a festive time. People went out to vote dressed in their best. Seeing them I too wanted to go and see a polling booth, and I accompanied Dadiji a few times. But most of the time I wasn't allowed because shootouts at these places were not uncommon.

9

I had now started being conscious of my religious identity. The first time I became aware of my religion was when I was told about a boy in another class being a Muslim. If he was Muslim, what was I? I was informed: Hindu. He was the only Muslim boy in our school, my senior, and I remember him because he used to play a lot of football. Those were the days before cricket and tennis became popular, when children played football, volleyball, kabaddi, *chhua-chhui*, etc. This boy could kick the ball really high and he was a well-known figure at school. People said that he was very strong because he was a Muslim and he ate meat. If meat could give so much energy, why didn't everyone eat it, I asked myself. My family did but most others did not.

I met the second Muslim in my life three years later at Sunrise Public School. The rickshaw that ferried kids to and from school was pulled by a man called Mohammed

Qasim. At the old school, my idea of a Muslim was someone with a beard and a cap who ate meat. Now I discovered that Muslims also pulled rickshaws. But others did too, so what was the difference?

I discovered this soon enough. In the summer months, school started early in the morning and classes were over by afternoon. On Fridays most children were taken by rickshaw to their homes but the rest of us had to wait for ours. That was when I learnt of one more point of difference – that Muslims went to the mosque and recited the namaz.

The differences were gradually becoming clear. Most Hindus didn't eat meat; Muslims did. We went to temples, Muslims to mosques. Their names were different from ours. By now these three broad distinctions were quite clear to me. Later on, one more was added to the list.

Pitaji had a very dear friend: Mohammed Jalaluddin. He was very well-off. I learnt then that some Muslims could also be rich and educated and teach in schools. Jalaluddinji's family lived in Saudi Arabia and they had expensive watches, radios and Walkmans, which really impressed us kids. The chocolates they got for us were also different. Most of our poor relatives gave us lemon drops, which we called lemonchoos or, worse still, nemonchoos, when they visited. Some who were better off got us good chocolates like the popular Morton bars. But Jalaluddinji always bought fancy Kismi Bars for us.

When he visited us he was taken inside to sit and he was fed well, usually meat or fish. This upset Dadiji, who was convinced that this was a blasphemous act. We didn't have a puja room but pictures of gods from cheap calendars had been framed and put up on the walls of the main room, which was Dadiji's sanctum sanctorum. She felt that her space was being polluted. Despite this, our relations with Jalaluddinji flourished. He continued to visit our home and later when I went to Patna I visited him and spent time with his family.

Deeper than religion was the consciousness of caste. With each passing day my understanding of caste deepened, and I didn't learn these lessons in school.

My first brush with caste was through colours. All of us children liked bright colours, but these were called 'shudra' (low-caste) colours. Later I often wondered about the irony of the fact that those who are themselves 'shudra' or low caste also used this terminology. Much later I realized that this is how deep-rooted cultural consciousness can be.

Our house had a *khaprail* roof, that is to say it was made of terracotta tiles. The first time I came to Delhi I was amazed to see people dancing joyfully in the rain. Back home, when the rains came, misery accompanied them.

To reduce the distance to school, we usually took a

shortcut through the fields, but if we did this in the rainy season we would get filthy with mud. Cooking fuel would get damp and created problems in the kitchen and we'd have to make do with *sattu* for dinner. Water dripped into the rooms through the roof, making it difficult to sleep. We didn't have enough utensils to place under all the leaking points. And so I never liked the rains.

The khaprail had to be repaired every year. The same person came to do this every year: Batoran Paswan. He was Dadaji's friend and I associated him with my grandfather. And so whenever Batoranji visited I'd stand up and offer him a seat.

Batoranji didn't have any one profession. During the harvest, he worked in the fields. At other times, he pulled a rickshaw. And in the monsoon, people called him to fix their roofs. In all these three professions he had a deep relationship with my family.

We owned very little land, and after the division following Dadaji's death this came down even further. But while he was alive there was substantial work to be done on the land and Batoranji took care of everything. When Dadaji had to go to the market or if we had to be given our polio vaccination, Batoranji took us in his rickshaw. After Dadaji passed away, Batoranji visited us only once a year – to fix the roof.

When Batoranji visited, I'd ask Ma to make tea for

him. She was more liberal than Dadiji, who used to get upset that I'd keep Batoranji's cup right next to the chullah with everybody else's. This bothered me. It also bothered me that he chose to sit on the floor even though I offered him my seat.

Children teased him and playfully called out 'Oye Batoran' to him whereas he used to address kids with more respect. At any public function, Batoranji and others of his caste were invariably the last to eat, and they had to then wash their own plates as no one else would touch any utensil from which they had eaten.

Things like this upset me. I had never seen any of my uncles or other members of the family washing their own dishes. But I felt upset not so much because of ideological convictions but because of my affection for him. My affection for Batoranji extended to his grandson, with whom I used to hang out to watch the popular serial *Chandrakanta*.

Our village had one library: Comrade Chandrashekhar Smarak Pustakalaya. People of all ages came here to read books and play carrom. The library hall also doubled up as a TV room and people from the village would gather around to watch serials. It was the time TV had made Ram the most popular deity in religious as well as political terms.

You could understand the social structure of the village

from observing such a gathering. The caste and economic status of viewers determined their distance from the TV set. The powerful sat close to it, and those who had neither power nor caste on their side settled down right at the back. Some homes in the village also had their own black-and-white TVs and this too attracted people from the neighbourhood. To the owners, televisions, telephones and cars served as possessions to make other people feel inferior.

Here too a similar kind of politics would play out. The children of people whose homes we visited to watch TV weren't friendly with children like me who came from poor families – their friends were other TV owners. I had to stand with the poor and their children. In our society the poor are the Dalits and the backward classes and it was with them that I stood at the door, balancing myself holding the window grill as I gazed at the screen. I may have been of a higher caste – we may not have had to wash our dishes – but in terms of my economic status I was no different from them.

10

It was in the year 2000 that I saw a cellphone for the first time. There was a wedding in the village. The bridegroom was an engineer in Delhi and the friend accompanying him had a cellphone. Instead of the groom, his friend became the centre of attraction.

The world around me was changing.

Under the communist influence some very positive attitudes were prevalent in the village. Boys and girls played kabaddi, football and volleyball together, or sat in the library side by side. The movement questioned orthodox thinking, encouraged widow remarriage and inter-caste marriage, opposed superstition, encouraged scientific thinking and worked against caste-based oppression. You can get an idea of the far-reaching effects of the movement by the fact that my bua, my father's sister, was married to a Dalit. The concept of honour killing doesn't exist there.

The sweep of globalization weakened this movement – many relics of the past started crumbling. Old factories shut down, trade unions were disbanded and the party lost its hold on my village. A new kind of politics emerged, which was fuelled by money and muscle power. In this race, the CPI got left behind.

The number of private schools was constantly on the rise. There was already a Dayanand Anglo-Vedic (DAV) school; now we also had St Paul's School, Mount Carmel and Lady Mariam Convent. There were many different kinds of education available for the same society. Schools were fashioned like shops. Some children went to schools where old jute sacks were used as floor mats to sit on in the classrooms. Those who were better off went to private schools, while the prosperous families sent their children to even fancier schools in the city. Huge school buses came to pick them up. We had heard that these schools were bigger than even some colleges.

Day-to-day life was also changing. Earlier, one would have to stand in a long queue to secure a cooking gas connection. Now there were private companies and gas became easily available. Where the Rajdoot motorcycle used to be the king of the road, now cars of various brands sped up and down. The markets were flooded with new products. Men usually wore shirts, but now T-shirts made their entry into the village, as did branded shoes. People's desires and aspirations were growing. The youth led this transformation.

These changes became clearer to me years later, when I began studying sociology. Old norms were giving way to new ideas and, seeing neighbours falling in love with each other in movies, boys and girls from different castes or living in the same locality began to look at each other in a new light – an unthinkable possibility just a few years ago.

The process of change was complex. On the one hand there was an unprecedented increase in consumables, and growing awareness too, but the situation on the ground was deteriorating. The youth had more dreams but fewer opportunities for employment.

Teaching jobs were available in schools but only on a contractual basis – regular appointments seemed to be a thing of the past. The other openings were in the armed forces. Boys practised running first thing in the morning to train for a life in the army but the recruitment process became a racket. Candidates had impostors run on their behalf and had to pay two lakh, sometimes three, to get in.

The looming threat of unemployment gave birth to a new wave of crime. There had always been a culture of violence in my village because of the feudal structure of the region. Disputes between two families over land were common. Sometimes when we were in school, we'd hear the sound of firing in the nearby fields and the teachers would keep all the children indoors.

Violence over land was an inseparable part of village life and I gradually became more aware of it. As I grew older it felt paradoxical that technology was growing and democracy was thriving but feudal forces continued to be strong. This holds even today. Though it cannot be said that we live in a feudal society, it also cannot be said that we don't.

In addition, the Congress had introduced a culture of violence into politics – one reason why I wasn't allowed out on polling day. All these factors had intensified. Earlier, the village panchayat had been made up of select educated and sober village elders who sorted out local issues and helped people. Now it was goons with rifles who people went to with their problems. This was a phase of terrible crime in the village – even small children walked around brandishing guns. There were thirty killings in the village in one month alone. Intoxicants were gaining popularity – there was a time when just a handful consumed alcohol, now there was just a handful who didn't.

Pitaji used to worry about how to keep me away from all this. But there was no way he could do that. One of Ma's uncles was a teacher at one of the better schools in the district. Radhakrishna Chamaria High School was a government school but the facilities there were no less than those of any St Paul's institution. It was three kilometres away and lay outside Masnadpur. Wanting me to stay away from the village as much as possible and concentrate on my studies, Pitaji decided to send me there.

So I was back at a government school. The first year I commuted by bus, which cost me two rupees per journey. After the first month, aping the other students, I stopped paying. Students never paid the bus fare. And because of our unity, the bus conductors let us be. Our argument was that the bus didn't move on fuel alone; it needed water too, for the radiator, that is. We told them to collect the fuel money from other passengers and that we would take care of the water. The four rupees we saved were spent on eating gol gappas.

Unlike Sunrise, I fit in at my new school easily – it had students from the same family background as me. I didn't feel so isolated here. I wasn't the butt of jokes because of my dress or style of speaking and I felt more at ease.

Besides, the standard of studies there was good. Even now, senior teachers in government schools don't teach history holding the textbook in their hands – they know their subject well. We had many such teachers in this school. And so, all things said, it was easy to study there.

My love of reading literature, however, affected my studies. While Premchand helped me understand the world, the fact that I strayed from the syllabus started reflecting in my performance. I was in class eight or nine by then and the school's lessons were not enough. Most students had to take private tuitions during this time. I asked Pitaji for extra lessons but he made it clear he couldn't afford it.

Then he found a way out. He suggested I leave home early every morning and go five kilometres to my grand-uncle and take extra coaching from him. Initially I was hesitant because it would mean going on the bus by myself and spending four rupees on the fare.

I suggested to Pitaji that if he were to buy me a cycle it would really help me and also save on bus money. He agreed. When I was in class nine I got my first cycle

When we talk of equality we must remember that there can be no equality of outcomes without the equality of resources and opportunities. When you don't get enough to eat at home and have to struggle to get everything, it'll definitely show in your performance.

Within three months, I fell sick. My routine of eating the previous night's roti in the morning, cycling five kilometres for tuition, staying without food till late afternoon and then cycling the same distance back had taken its toll on me. I had to give up my morning tuition yet again. My association with maths started to come to an end. We had to do algebra now, which was impossible to understand without tuition. Soon, science and maths started appearing tougher than conquering the Everest.

But social sciences continued to be my strong point. Extra reading and life experiences helped in developing a sound understanding of these subjects and high scores in these made it possible for me to continue doing well in school.

11

The years that followed were very difficult for my family. When I was in class nine, my sister got married. Because Pitaji had no savings he had to mortgage a small portion of family land where our home stood. In our country, land is not sold or mortgaged to educate girls, but for their marriage. Didi was taking the class ten exam and Jijaji was in class twelve. Marriage at such a young age was illegal but this was how things were in our villages.

My family's finances were at an all-time low. Earlier, we bought atta by the sackful; now we could barely afford the small polythene bags of atta. It was considered a shame for an upper-caste farming family to buy atta, not to mention small bags of it. The constant worries about money scarred me. I felt my dreams becoming smaller and smaller.

I used to love cricket but once I moved back to the government school, I had to give up that love. I couldn't even think of buying a bat – one cost five hundred rupees. I now knew it was a game for the rich and that we could only play kabaddi, which cost nothing. I felt I wouldn't be able to join the exciting professions I craved and be an engineer, doctor or district collector.

I thought of giving up studies. My older brother had already done so and had started working as a guard in a factory in Guwahati, Assam. I was in class ten and I wondered what use school could be for me when there were no opportunities.

But I liked to study and wasn't very strong physically. I wanted to take up something where I could keep up with my reading, rather than being a guard or mechanic, or running a provision store where physical labour was needed. I thought of taking up a job at a bookstore. There was one such shop in our market: Lekhni Pustak Bhandar.

This shop sold books and the owner had expanded and started selling fans and bulbs too. He was looking for an assistant. I spoke to the owner, suggesting that he allow me to work in the books' section. It was settled – I was to get five hundred rupees a month. I was very excited.

But I never got down to starting it. It so happened that I got a job where, for fifty rupees a day, I had to go from house to house and give polio drops to children. This work was easier because it hardly took any of my time and the money was almost the same. I had some fascinating experiences because of this job.

People were apprehensive of polio drops because it was widely believed that they consisted of a medicine that caused impotency and the government was cleverly feeding them to children as a population control measure. Many bluntly refused to allow their kids to take the drops. But we had strict instructions to administer them to all children below the age of five. Parents would sign on our sheet without letting us administer the drops to the children. In our country schemes run on such fake signatures. When we reached schools at the lunch break to give the drops, children would run away at the sight of us.

Eventually, Pitaji came to know of my job. It set him thinking. He had no good reason for stopping me because he too had no idea what I would be doing in the future. Nonetheless, he asked me to concentrate on the class ten exams in the coming months, and start working after they ended. Perhaps he thought that this way I wouldn't be in a position to say that I was made to work at the cost of my studies. Perhaps he wanted to free himself of this possible guilt.

What Pitaji didn't realize was that if my primary and middle-level education was sound, then clearing the Bihar Board exams would not be so difficult. The only subject that frightened me was maths, but I managed to score forty-seven out of hundred in it. In all the other subjects I scored good marks. I did very well in the social sciences and my highest score was in Sanskrit. Actually, this was thanks to the nervousness of the Sanskrit teachers who marked the papers liberally, fearing that being stingy with marks would mean that the students would avoid Sanskrit altogether. I passed class ten with a first division.

When the result was announced, Pitaji was in hospital. He had fallen sick right after my exams, diagnosed with diabetes. The hospital bills would have ruined us had it not been for the fact that he fell ill during a family wedding where all our relatives got together and took care of the expense.

I used to stay in the hospital to take care of Pitaji, leaving his side only when I had to go out to bring tea, medicines, etc. One day when I went out to get tea I saw that the class ten results had come out in the papers. In my eagerness to see the result I paid the vendor five rupees instead of three rupees and fifty paise. I began frantically searching in the columns of roll numbers under the third division, where I did not find mine. With a pounding heart I moved to the second division and finally to the first division dreading I had failed.

When I saw my score, I was on cloud nine. This was not the first time that I had got a first division but it had come at exactly the right time, when I was wondering about the point of studying, secretly fearing that I might fail because of the lack of tuitions.

In the hospital ward, I informed Pitaji that the result was out. Worried, he asked me what it was in an uncertain tone. I tried to sound calm. 'I've got first division.' But he was not satisfied, always ready for bad news. 'How many marks in science?'

The result was good for me, but not so good for the school. Only twenty-seven students got a first division as against seventy or eighty in previous years. So when I went to collect my mark sheet I found the office peon in a foul mood. He asked me for a tip. I told him I didn't even have money for the bus. He scolded me, 'Don't ruin my mood first thing in the morning. As it is very few have done well this year so there'll be hardly any tips. And here you are, a first division, actually saying no!'

I asked him to keep my mark sheet if he liked but I had no money to give him. While we were still arguing, one of my teachers walked by. He asked the peon not to bother me, saying that I genuinely didn't have money. With a heavy heart, the peon held out the mark sheet towards me, saying, 'What are you going to do with a first division anyway?'

He was right. What was I going to do with a first division?

Pitaji's reaction to my result was mixed. Fighting a long

illness and debt, he had received some good news after ages, one that he had given up hope on. It made him very happy. But deep inside he was also worried that now he'd have to do something more for me. After a good result it would be cruel to ask me to go and work at Lekhni Pustak Bhandar. His duty towards my education had always been a burden to him and the noose had just become tighter.

But for me the result was liberating. My old doubts were gone. I knew I had to study further and not take up a job. The only worry was figuring out what my next step should be. At the district level, there were still only government colleges; private colleges had not yet made inroads. In Begusarai, Bihar, GD College was a well-known institution. Everyone advised me to go there for intermediate studies.

I knew, however, that if I were to follow this path, my options would once again be limited. I had had a taste of the lawless culture of these campuses in my years at government schools. That is to say, in the first year, sit inside the bus, in the second year, sit on top of the bus, and in the third year, burn the bus. I thought that after this what was bound to follow was the firing of guns. Did I want to take that path?

There were only two factors that could have saved me from such a future, and I've mentioned them earlier. One, I was physically weak, and two, I was interested in political and cultural activities and loved literature.

No, I didn't want to study in Begusarai. Hesitantly, I told Pitaji that I wanted to go to Patna instead. It was only in the capital city that I could be free of the complex, stifling ties of my village life. Pitaji was in a quandary – it was very expensive to live and study in Patna. I told him I had spoken to some people and been told that I'd need only five hundred rupees a month.

For the first time, I saw Pitaji seized with a passion. Despite his illness, he started going to work every morning. It was a great effort on his part. If he hadn't been so motivated, I could never have studied beyond class ten. He managed the impossible and raised the money.

With this, my days in the village came to an end. Carrying my bedding, a small gas cylinder – which was sometimes used at home for making tea – and some food, I left for Patna.

Part 2

Patna

12

It was a humid August day when I reached Patna. The sun was just beginning to set. This had been the longest journey of my life. While waiting for the train at Gadhara I had been tempted to save eighteen rupees and travel without a ticket. But the fear of the penalty had made me buy one. I needn't have bothered. When the train arrived I couldn't find a place in the compartment and had to squeeze in somehow.

In Patna I disembarked, dazed and excited. I couldn't believe I was in this huge city. Much to the disappointment of the rickshaw-wallahs who hungrily approached me, I walked across a maze of railway tracks and found my way to Mitthu Lodge, where I was going to stay.

As was the common practice in Patna, this lodge with a khaprail roof rented out bedding, not rooms. The bedding that I had chosen cost me two hundred and fifty rupees a month. My room had one more occupant. He showed me my corner, his tone smacking of ownership.

I made myself busy arranging my things, setting up a home in the corner of the room. I had brought some food supplies – five kilos of atta bought from a shop back home, to be paid for later; one litre of mustard oil; one bar of soap for washing clothes; one bathing soap; one brush; one tongue cleaner; Colgate; the gas burner which Ma had reluctantly parted with; and a new bed sheet she had stitched together with bits and pieces of old fabric.

The Patna outside my room felt not just big but slightly frightening. All my life I had seen cattle and birds looking for food in garbage heaps. For the first time now I was seeing children and adults scavenging for food. So this was what a twentieth-century city of India looked like. Until I came to Delhi, Patna would remain for me the ultimate metropolis.

This was also the first time that I had to take decisions entirely on my own. I had to make my own arrangements for studies, meals and clothes. At home Ma and Pitaji were always there. Here there was no one. But it's easy to make decisions when there are very few options available to you.

In Bihar, if you had done well in maths in class ten you opted for engineering. If you did well in biology, you studied medicine. Very few people chose the humanities.

That was how careers were decided and there were no alternatives. My maths was better than biology, even though I had struggled with it in my class ten boards, and so I decided to become an engineer.

After zeroing in on the stream of subjects all one had to do was find the right coaching institute. Stand on a road in Patna and throw a stone in any direction, it's bound to land either on a coaching institute or on its hoarding – or so the joke went. From the bustling Ashok Rajpath and its surrounding areas to Rajendra Nagar Nala Road where the big train station stood, coaching institutes had mushroomed all over the city. Though they offered hardly anything by way of infrastructure or resources, the fees were very high. For poor students like me they were out of reach so this choice was also taken out of my hands.

But I was very keen to study further and was determined to find the means to do so.

I chose not a coaching institute but a maths tuition class. My roommate had studied with a tutor called Abhimanyu sir and I went to meet him to be interviewed. Abhimanyu sir's interest in me perked up on hearing the name of my village. He asked what my family did and became even more excited when I told him that Dadaji and Pitaji worked at the Barauni Thermal Power Plant at Bihat.

As luck would have it, he knew my father. Actually his

71

older brother worked at the thermal power station and Abhimanyu sir had lived there with him to study. As the family weren't from Bihat, they were considered outsiders, while Pitaji was of course a local person. Outsiders and locals led contrasting lives – no one troubles the locals while outsiders are often harassed. Pitaji had always come to Abhimanyu sir's and his brother's rescue and helped them out of tricky situations. So his entire family was very grateful to him. My surprise arrival had given them the chance to return the gesture – my fee was waived off. I felt like the luckiest boy in the world.

But my luck didn't hold out in my living arrangements. My roommate's attitude towards me was very hostile in a passive-aggressive way. He considered the room to be his property simply because he had arrived first. I had to take his permission before doing anything, though this didn't soften his behaviour. We were distantly related and my bua had done him a favour which had led to him offering me a space in his room. But he was clearly resentful of my presence and always made sure to make me feel obliged.

If I wanted to study late at night I'd have to buy a table lamp, he told me, because he couldn't sleep with the light on. But when he wanted to read, I was to get used to sleeping with the light on. Food and my gas burner helped thaw our relations somewhat. We made an arrangement to share the cooking. I was to cook a vegetable dish at night, and he agreed to make rotis since I didn't know how to make them properly. And so our partnership fell uneasily into place.

This was the first time I was away from home, living with a stranger, following the rules laid down by him. My distance from my roommate and his unreasonable rules and regulations brought me closer to others. I made friends with a boy who lived in the same lodge and started spending time with him. This too annoyed my roommate. It was obvious this arrangement couldn't last for long.

So this was my new life. Wake up, have breakfast – either biscuits or chana soaked overnight. Lunch comprised rice, dal and aloo ka chokhaa – a simple preparation of boiled potatoes. All these were cooked together in the pressure cooker using a separator. Potatoes appeared again for dinner, with the dal and rice replaced by rotis.

The lodge was a tiny, cramped place with no ventilation. It held fifty boys and had only one toilet, leading to long queues. In summer it was insufferably hot and we were always drenched in sweat. The Patna heat is very humid, especially after the rains. At night after cooking dinner we would have to bathe before we could bring ourselves to eat.

To save myself from the endless toilet queue, I changed my routine. I'd wake up after everyone had left for tuition.

But water was available only at fixed times and by the time I was up the taps would have run dry and I'd have to wait till the afternoon to bathe.

I gradually settled into my new life. Of the money I got from home, two hundred and fifty rupees went towards the lodge rent. The remaining amount was used for buying necessities, which I made sure I bought from the cheapest place. Sabzi-wallahs usually cheat on quantity, especially while selling to students. A friendship was developed with one seller and he eventually started giving me the correct amount – 3 kilos of potatoes for what he used to quote as the price of two and a half kilos.

This way I managed to save some more money. I struck a bargain at Ashok Rajpath and bought a pair of shorts – or half pant as we called them – for twenty-five rupees. This was what I wore at the lodge – a half pant and a vest. For going out I had only two sets of clothes – wear one, wash one.

I mostly walked to wherever I had to go. I couldn't afford an auto or a rickshaw. Then one day I found a cycle. A relative in the city had an old cycle at their place, obvious from its condition that no one used it. They also had an old typewriter. As I was leaving I asked them for both these things. They didn't give me the typewriter but parted with the cycle.

13

Alongside my maths lessons, I had taken admission in the intermediate course in a high school called Ram Ratan Mahavidyalaya, Patna. But I never attended a single class. Like countless others who joined coaching classes for engineering I went there only to get enrolled, take the exam and collect the result when it was declared.

The college admission only ensured that I would be able to take my intermediate exams. But it was the coaching classes that one needed to attend to actually learn the engineering syllabus. Since I couldn't afford the engineering tutorials, I spent most of my time in my room studying on my own. I owned very few books and usually borrowed from my roommate.

But the maths classes weren't going well. Every morning I'd get ready for the tutorial with a heavy heart. The thought of parabola and ellipses made me feel almost dizzy with worry. With every passing day, with each new lesson, the language of mathematics felt more and more incomprehensible. Instead of being given the key to learning, it felt as if a new lock was put on the door each day.

My confidence dropped. My anxiety was similar to what I used to feel in the Sunrise Public School days. The resources were few, the challenges many. After much time and effort, I had managed to overcome the challenges there. But what I was now faced with seemed beyond my capabilities. I simply couldn't learn engineering without taking expensive coaching classes. I'd thought hard work and discipline would get me through but life's experiences had taught me time and time again that simply making up one's mind to do well is not enough. Good intentions need a support system too.

Within a year I knew that I couldn't cope with the studies for the engineering entrance exam. It wasn't possible for me to attend the intermediate classes and I didn't have money to pay for more coaching. I couldn't even afford to buy the textbooks. So how could I aspire to be an engineer? Perhaps I should never have taken up this subject.

Filled with doubt and worry, I poured my heart out to Pitaji. Then I went to my tutor and thanked him for his efforts at drilling maths into me. I said I had understood nothing and requested them to let me leave the centre. We parted as friends. But what of my future?

For the poor, dreams and reality are two banks of a river which never meet. When I had come to Patna I didn't know my life was going to play out like this. I was trying to swim across to the other side of the river but the current was pulling me back to where I started from.

14

With no clear path ahead, I assessed my situation as calmly as I could. I felt I couldn't study any more. The purpose of studying seemed to be only to make money. But in the India I encountered, engineers were jobless and MBA graduates sold detergent. And in any case you needed money to make money. Was it not better to think of some other way of making a living – somewhere abroad, for instance?

Pitaji's friend Mohammed Jalaluddin lived in the city of Nawada, about a hundred kilometres from Patna. He was one of the few family friends we had who was successful and well-off, having made money in the Gulf. Jalaluddinji used to tell Pitaji that it was quite easy to get a visa for Dubai if one had knowledge of any technical work. I thought that if I were to learn how to repair air conditioners and fridges, I could find employment in Dubai. I deferred paying the rent for the lodge for that month and saved on some other expenses to put together five hundred rupees to pay for an AC–fridge repair course. I also decided to pay Jalaluddinji a visit in his hometown to take his advice on getting to Dubai.

I was shocked on seeing his house for the first time. Jalaluddinji, who used to humbly take off his shoes before entering our small home in the village, lived in a palatial mansion, the sight of which took my breath away.

There was a cricket match between India and Pakistan on the day of my visit. We were sitting in the outer part of the house while the TV was inside. Like others I too was interested in the match and so kept asking for the score. Seeing my interest Jalaluddinji asked me if I'd like to come inside to see the match. As we entered the room, the women of the family sitting close to the TV got up and left but the boys and girls continued to sit and watch the match.

Pakistan had finished batting and had scored very well. The locality had already let loose one round of firecrackers to celebrate their performance. India started batting. There was a cute four-year-old among the viewers. Sachin was batting and every time he took a run the boy looked upset.

During the break when we stepped out I asked him, 'Who is your favourite player?'

He said, 'Shahid Afridi.'

'Why?'

'He plays very well.'

'Sachin also plays very well.'

'After Shahid I like Sachin.'

'So, in this match today, who do you want to win?'

'Shahid Afridi.'

'Why?'

A shadow crossed the boy's face. He said, 'If Sachin wins, you will get an answer to your why.'

I was struck by the seriousness of his reply but got my answer as soon as the match ended. India had won and jeering local supporters began to throw burning firecrackers into Jalaluddinji's house. It didn't feel like a celebration; it felt like war. As I watched the mayhem in astonishment, the little boy came to stand next to me. He asked, 'Now you know why I like Shahid Afridi?'

That night when I narrated the story to Jalaluddinji he said, 'He doesn't want to like Shahid but is forced to… he has no choice.' I realized then how entrenched the communalization of cricket in this country is.

Years later, on a trip to Kashmir for a seminar, I was struck by this phenomenon once again. I was travelling from Srinagar to Sonmarg and on the way I saw many cricket matches being held in open grounds. In some, I noticed that one of the teams wore the same uniform as that of the Pakistan cricket team. The other team's uniforms didn't have India written on them but were of a similar blue.

I was puzzled. When we reached Sonmarg, a match was under way. I asked a local boy about the mystery of the Pakistan uniform.

The boy said, 'By the looks of you, you appear to be an educated person.'

'Yes.'

'Don't you know, your enemy's enemy is a friend?'

'Then why is the other team wearing blue?'

'This is a rule. The host team always wears Pakistan's uniform. And the opposing or guest team has to wear blue.'

So this was the politics of cricket and the cricket of politics.

That night at Jalaluddinji's house was an eye-opener in more ways than one. He told me that as soon as I found a job in the Gulf, my family's days of poverty would be a thing of the past. That even after spending freely from my salary I'd still have at least fifty to sixty thousand rupees to send home.

I had been feeling helpless and lost. His words gave me a new strength. I realized that whatever I wanted to do in life, I had to achieve it on my own. No one else was going to take decisions about me. If any risks were involved, I'd take them myself. I returned from Nawada full of enthusiasm and now eagerly went for my training, scrimping and saving to make sure I could pay my fees.

15

It had now been close to two years since I came to Patna. I was becoming a Patna boy, that is to say I was turning into a high-flyer.

I began to travel in trains without buying a ticket. Then it struck me that if I was caught I'd be fined anyway, so why travel in the ordinary coach? And so I started using the AC coach. If a ticket collector asked to check my ticket I answered him so boldly that he, unwilling to pick a fight, would just move on.

I began to hang out at roadside stalls with friends, drinking tea and arguing about politics – a Patna obsession. Politics is at the very core of life in Bihar. Whether it is a tea shop or a paan shop, a roundabout or inside a train, within five minutes of meeting people are discussing politics. In fact, in Patna, if you're in a rickshaw and if the ride is longish, within ten minutes the rickshaw-wallah will turn the rickshaw into a prime-time newsroom.

My circle of friends and acquaintances too was expanding. My closest friend in Mitthu Lodge was a boy called Manibhushan. He was completing his BA from Patna University in Urdu. He was an interesting fellow, a Hindu who was studying Urdu. In his company I started reading literature once again; I had dropped my habit since moving to the big city. Manibhushan was also politically inclined. After the 2002 riots a fact-finding team had gone to Gujarat and he had accompanied them. He was full of stories about the BJP's atrocities in the state and made me dislike the right-wing party even more.

I didn't have the money to buy newspapers, so I read them at Manibhushan's place. He used to buy the local Hindi paper. But I was constantly being told that to be successful it was important to read the newspaper in English. I had never understood how students who started with 'This is a cat' in class six could be expected to start reading fluently in English as soon as they passed class ten. And yet nothing seemed possible without English.

Since I couldn't afford it, Manibhushan showed me a place where the English paper would be delivered. It was a tiny house tucked away in the area, close to Mitthu Lodge. At first I thought it was a private residence. I thought Manibhushan was teasing me. 'I'm sure many homes get the English newspaper. So should I walk into people's homes and start reading the paper?' I asked my friend indignantly.

But he corrected me: this was not a home, it was an office of the Communist Party of India. And anyone could walk in to read books and newspapers there.

I was reminded of an occasion when I was walking on the road and was very thirsty. Seeing a bank, I decided to go inside to drink water. The guard let me in but when I walked towards the water he stopped me. The water was for customers only.

This was the humanitarian face of globalization.

I became a regular at the CPI office. Every Friday, they held a study circle. Mani used to attend these sessions and I too decided to participate. The faces in the study circle were familiar. There were some people from the IPTA with whom I had interacted in Begusarai as well as a few lawyers, some students and one old man. I had often seen him making speeches in my village. He was called Shiv Shankar Sharma and he frequently spoke against the BJP as a party that used religion to realize its political ambitions.

In the early days I was mostly quiet in the study circle. Books like Lenin's *Imperialism: The Highest Stage of Capitalism* were discussed. I didn't understand everything and, feeling shy, just used to listen quietly to what was being said. A friend from the study circle was sympathetic to my plight. He took me to a bookshop and introduced me to simpler books of illustrated Soviet stories. In Begusarai it was literature and social sciences that I most loved studying and now I returned to these, reading novels, history, politics. Slowly, invisibly, my horizons were beginning to expand.

My head had always had two warring sides and the battle between them now intensified. One side worried about my family. Pitaji's financial situation was moving from bad to worse and I was beginning to feel cornered. I knew I had to find a job fairly soon. And yet the other part of me was beginning to ask larger and larger questions. Some of these were to do with my future and my ambitions for myself, the others were a continuation of the questions I had started asking in the village.

The question of identity really obsessed me at the time. In Patna I felt like a perpetual outsider, always a little out of step with the world, someone unnecessary and unwanted. Being an outsider in fact was a theme of my years in the city. I was made to feel an outsider by my roommate; I didn't have the resources to study properly; in my first year I felt I had barely any friends. The system felt unforgiving and there was no one to help.

As I thought more deeply, I realized that I had always been an outsider wherever I had studied, other than at my first school. I had been made to feel it too. Meanwhile, nationally, the question of Bihari identity had become a politically sensitive subject. The Maharashtra regional chauvinist party Shiv Sena was forcing migrants from Bihar and Uttar Pradesh to leave the state, arguing that they were taking over the jobs of poor, ordinary Maharashtrians. I felt that those who discriminated against me here for being an outsider would themselves get beaten up if they were to go to Maharashtra. Perhaps everyone was an outsider at some time or the other. But the poor were the most so.

I saw the way poverty had given me such few choices. I began to think of what it had done to others. Religion was the traditional shelter of the poor. But I had become detached from religion. I had recently read a book by Swami Vivekananda in which he said that to talk of religion to the poor was an irreligious thing to do. Those words burned in my mind.

16

The results of my intermediate exam came in. I had passed with a second division. In the village, such a result would have upset me. But in Patna it filled me with hope. The centre allocated to me for the exam was a hub for cheating. A comprehensive answer key called 'atom bomb' was available to us students and everyone used it freely to copy answers. I was the only student who didn't cheat and I had been mocked by my friends for playing it so straight. Yet, surprisingly, when our results came in, every student in my college got a second division whether they had cheated or not. It made me feel I had a chance to do things my way.

The result filled me with new motivation and I began to wonder if Dubai was the right route for me. As the plan stood now I'd go to Dubai, make money, help my family, start using the kind of things Jalaluddinji's family did, and give gifts to friends and relatives. But when

I returned to my village and people asked me what I did, would I simply say I fixed ACs and refrigerators? Would that answer satisfy me? These last few years in Patna had opened my horizons and given me greater ambition.

In Bihar, the touchstone of success is a car with a beacon. Young people want to become IAS officers and dream of walking with personal security, driving in a car with a red beacon on top, and being saluted wherever they go. In our world, the status of an IAS officer is way above that of someone who repairs ACs and fridges.

I did not realize then that a doctor and a sweeper are equally important in running a hospital. The absence of any one of them makes proper functioning impossible. I decided to continue my studies and join a BA course at a college, and prepare for the nationwide UPSC exam alongside, my route to enter the civil services. I would pay for my expenses by giving tuitions. This would not only bring me a high-status job and a good income but it might be more suited to my talents.

The long political reign of Lalu Prasad Yadav and his wife Rabri Devi as chief ministers was coming to an end. After many years, the politics of Patna and the entire state was changing. My generation had grown up in a globalized world and dreamt of making it big. We were now looking for options. But there were no fresh avenues and no new choices. Jobs continued to be elusive, and higher education held no promise.

Government jobs were fast depleting, villages were deteriorating and farmers and others who worked with their hands survived on hope and hope alone. There was disillusionment all around and very little happening to bring about a change. In such a situation there was a rat race among the youth for the few remaining government openings. Nursing the UPSC dream, I too had become part of it.

I was determined to join a college where classes were actually held. I hadn't attended any classes in my intermediate school and this had affected my performance. I chose Commerce College, Patna. My subjects were geography (honours), history, sociology, Hindi and English. I had no particular interest in these subjects, but that year a twenty-two-year-old boy had topped the UPSC exam. He was the youngest topper ever and his subjects were geography and Hindi literature. And so I opted for those too. Other than these I had to take two more subjects and I chose sociology and history. History was considered a must for cracking the civil service exams. In those days people chose subjects for their study after reading winners' interviews in magazines like *Pratiyogita Darpan*.

On my first day at college I encountered a student

demonstration. The boy who was leading it was also a part of the study circle. He too had recognized me and was equally surprised to see me there. His name was Vishwajeet.

Vishwajeet was holding a flag which had AISF (All India Students' Federation) written on it. This was a national students' union, and the student wing of the CPI. I was familiar with the organization. In the study circle, I had attended its programme about education in Bihar and its challenges. I have to admit I had been less interested in the AISF speeches than the food that was to follow. But at the end, when only puri-sabzi packets were handed out, I had come away disappointed.

Later, Vishwajeet asked me to become a member of the AISF. I told him I was preparing for the UPSC exam and wouldn't have time for party activities. He said I need not devote any time and that I should continue to focus on studies but that one had to fight along with studying.

I couldn't understand what he was saying. Fight for what? He talked of the poor state of affairs in the college. There was no bathroom, no library, girls were harassed. It was important to fight for these things. These aspects didn't seem like reason enough to join but eventually I agreed. The AISF was after all the country's oldest student organization.

I started participating in some AISF activities,

especially seminars and discussions. I had always loved listening to speeches and taking part in debates at school. I became active again in the college debating society, rediscovering my love for it, and once again coming first.

The secret to being a good debater and public speaker is to know how to communicate with those directly in front of you. I felt that I should connect to others on the basis of what I myself had thought and experienced rather than spout empty words from a book that had no relevance to me. A person could not live in isolation in society. He had to be connected to the world and this was done through one's thoughts and actions. A farmer grew foodgrain, a worker produced goods, and great artists, writers and politicians connected to people by expressing their deepest selves.

During debates the most useful skill you can possess is the ability to gauge the mood of the audience and make your point accordingly. The purpose of a debate is to present your arguments and as far as possible make people see your point of view and agree with it. I always tried to see what the mood of the audience was and if they seemed to disagree with me on some point, I spent my time thinking about how I could change their minds. How could I not put them off, instead slowly bring them to my side? It was like a battle of minds in which I had to gauge what was in the mind of not only my opponents but also the audience in advance.

Debating made me a well-known face in college. After a long time, I achieved something that made life easier. In Patna I was ignored and anonymous. Seeing my slight frame, clerks in government offices would shoo me away. But now people would look at me differently. The fact that I was in the AISF also made some wary of me. The principal often lectured me to concentrate on my studies and stay away from the jhola-wallahs, trying to convince me that politics was a waste of time.

I believed him for a while but when the state government changed and his own principalship went with it I understood exactly what politics he was playing with me. As was true for most officials in lucrative posts, he was a supporter of the Rashtriya Janata Dal (RJD) and when the Janata Dal (U) came to power he was transferred to another post. When you are yourself a product of politics, to ask others to stay away from it is the most vicious and dangerous game you can play.

17

Through it all, I focused on my studies. An alumnus of the college used to coach students for competitive exams. I asked to study under him but also made it clear that I had no money to pay. He was generous and allowed me nonetheless to attend his classes.

Most of my free time, though, was taken up in teaching and not being taught. I gave tuitions in history, geography and sociology and was paid by the hour, fifteen rupees for one hour – this was the fee for teaching in Hindi. If I were to teach the same subjects in English I could earn twenty-seven rupees per hour.

And so time passed. My life now was a combination of studies, activism and tuitions. I managed to earn enough to meet my expenses. How the three years flew by is a mystery, and before I knew it I had completed BA in the first division and it was time to apply for my MA.

I couldn't join regular MA classes and decided to

pursue my course through distance learning while tutoring alongside. I enrolled at Nalanda Open University and took up sociology. I was also beginning to reconsider the UPSC decision. It was becoming increasingly clear to me that after joining the system, it would not be feasible to do social service. It's not possible to bring about a change once one is part of the system.

Despite my doubts, I stayed on the course I had decided. What preoccupied me more were the old worries: the dilemma of earning money and meeting my expenses. I was told that if I were to take tuitions in Delhi for the same subjects I could earn a thousand rupees. This would allow me to pay my way and also afford UPSC coaching classes, while studying for my MA through the open university. Delhi began to seem more and more attractive.

It is rightly said that your future is decided by the path you leave behind. I had left my village because I didn't want to be caught in the quagmire of unemployment and crime. Patna showed me the way forward. But now even the Patna sky felt limiting. Maybe it was because once you leave home you try to get to the best possible destination that you can reach.

Moreover, while Patna had given me a taste of the world outside Begusarai, not only was it near my home but culturally too there wasn't a big difference between the city and my village. In Patna too I was usually surrounded by people who knew my family from before.

Going to Delhi meant cutting myself off from all these ties. It actually meant going to an unknown place for the first time. Emotionally, it would mean breaking free from my family. Where I had been and where I was going were going to be completely different and I wasn't even sure if I could afford such a move.

I had to make my family understand this. But for them it made little difference whether I was in Patna or in Delhi as long as I took care of my educational needs. I think they were assured that whatever I was doing was after due deliberation.

And so I left for Delhi in 2009. I carried a lot of baggage on my trip – a computer, my books and, above all, the big hungry dream to go to the country's capital and study, teach and become someone in life.

Part 3
Delhi

18

There is a Patna–Delhi train called Sampoorna Kranti. The phrase, meaning 'total revolution', was the slogan of the great political leader Jayaprakash Narayan (popularly known as JP), coined during his fiery opposition to then prime minister Indira Gandhi in the 1970s. JP's total revolution never came, but his followers started a train with this name and nowadays people travel on the train and discuss the politics that began during the JP movement. And his shadow still looms large, with many political leaders today tracing their roots back to him. And so it was fitting that I boarded the Sampoorna Kranti one hot July day to my new home, Delhi.

The journey to the capital city was full of political discussions. The newly elected Congress coalition group, UPA-II, was in power but the country was witnessing massive anti-government feelings. Those who supported the government preferred to remain quiet but the rest of us in the coach were vocal. These days, however, the situation is the reverse. Those who are critical of the government prefer to remain quiet.

We were discussing many things – in particular, youth unemployment and the high rate of farmer suicides in the countryside. The government had waived off farmers' debts the previous year but, despite this, the suicides were rampant. The debate around achieving a national economic growth of two digits was at its loudest. In this country, the only index that matters is the stock market index (Sensex). Indexes of unemployment and farmer suicides ruin millions of lives but this grief does not penetrate the thick hide of those in charge of the economy of the country.

When the train reached New Delhi railway station, I looked around for a coolie. But I didn't have to call out for one. Instead, one came to me. When a coolie makes the first move, his attitude towards his customer is different. But not in my case. Seeing all my luggage and my young, vulnerable appearance, he quoted a sum that I could not afford. I looked around in despair and saw a trolley carrying large parcels. I approached the trolley puller and he agreed to take my luggage outside the station at a lower price.

Just as I was stepping out, a woman came up to me,

taking out a tiny tricolour with a charkha on it from her pocket. I stopped her. On my last visit a woman had pinned a similar flag on me and then demanded ten rupees for it. This time I was alert; I simply refused. And I felt rather pleased with myself. I had been to Delhi a few times before – for college and AISF trips. I felt I knew the ways of this city. No one could dupe me.

The station exit was buzzing with auto drivers. I had to go to Dwarka Mor in west Delhi to drop off my things with an acquaintance. After that I wanted to look for accommodation in Mukherjee Nagar. A neighbourhood in North Delhi, this was located fairly close to Delhi University (DU) and was the hub of UPSC coaching centres. While making my plans in Patna I had thought that living near these centres would make my preparations for the exam easier.

The auto drivers were asking for three hundred and fifty rupees. I was stunned. My journey from Patna had cost me the same amount. When I said this to the driver, I was told, 'It'll be three hundred and fifty rupees… nothing less. If you can't afford to travel in Delhi, you'd better go back to Patna.' I could not understand where this was coming from: was it sarcasm or the arrogance of a metropolitan city?

All the other autos quoted the same price. Seeing no other way out, I agreed. My feeling of triumph was quickly beginning to turn to confusion and irritation. This was the nation's capital and people came here from all over the world. To my eyes, it was full of mystery and intrigue. Even if one were to come here three hundred times it would still be a challenge to figure out how the city worked.

The feeling of being defeated by the big city intensified. Sitting in the auto, I discovered that the man I had made the deal with was different from the man who was actually driving the auto. I asked the driver who the other man was and he told me he was the tout whose job it was to settle the fare with customers. Passengers with too much luggage couldn't leave their belongings just anywhere and go looking for an auto. And the auto-wallahs couldn't leave their autos to go looking for passengers. And so this man did the needful and took a hundred rupees for every deal.

I also discovered that I hadn't been especially clever about using the trolley puller at the station. In his spare time, he often did this and carried the luggage straight to the tout. He also knew that the passenger couldn't go very far with so much luggage. From the trolley puller to the auto driver, everyone was playing his part to perfection and swindling me in the bargain.

Thus I came to understand how vested interests and businesses forged a nexus to keep prices up. Customers were swindled at every stage but the arrangements were such that you never realized you were being taken for a ride.

But my bitterness melted away when I learnt that the auto driver was from Muzaffarpur in Bihar. I felt a closeness towards him in the strange place. More than half the auto-wallahs in Delhi are from Bihar.

That evening, I went to Mukherjee Nagar. I was keen to find a room of my own as soon as possible. This time I took a DTC (run by the Delhi government) bus. After being tricked twice in a day, I was determined not to be played a third time. Public transport options like DTC buses and the Metro do not usually swindle passengers. Living in a city like Delhi, I've come to believe that in this country the struggle to keep the public sector alive is a fight for the rights of Dalits and the poor. That day if I had been in a private bus I could well have been swindled once again.

I got off at the GTB Nagar Metro station. From there I had been told to take a shared auto headed for Batra cinema, a landmark in the area. I didn't know that every passenger had to pay a fixed amount of five rupees. Getting off at Mukherjee Nagar, I routinely asked the driver how much I had to pay. He looked at me in a calculating manner, realizing I was new to the area. I could see he was wondering if he could use my ignorance to cheat me. Luckily I saw all the others paying five rupees each and, doing the same, I walked away.

I had been advised that the best way of finding a room in Mukherjee Nagar was through a property dealer. I saw several of them advertising their business. I found one thing strange, though. Why did someone who facilitated getting rented accommodation call himself a property dealer? Where was the property here? Most of us in this neighbourhood were looking for a simple room to rent. At best they could be called shelter dealers.

I approached a dealer. He wanted to know my budget. I could pay up to two thousand rupees. He said rentals in this locality were higher and suggested nearby areas like Gandhi Vihar, Nehru Vihar, Indira Vihar and Bhai Parmanand Colony.

He took me to Nehru Vihar. When people from Bihar set out for Mukherjee Nagar, they end up in the sewers of Nehru Vihar in the clutches of property dealers who offer uninhabitable places at unbelievable rates. But I didn't know this at the time.

While looking at rooms in Nehru Vihar, I noticed some advertisements. I love reading ordinary-looking advertisements pasted on to walls. These are the billboards of the poor. Most of the flyers were of tuition classes but I was intrigued by some that said 'Need a room partner' or 'Need a girl room partner'. I wondered if the first one meant that both boys and girls were acceptable, and I thought this hinted at a very liberal environment.

One advertisement caught my eye. It was the only flyer that also mentioned the rent – three thousand two hundred rupees. I thought that the person who had written such a notice must be sensible and direct. I made some excuse to the property dealer and as soon as he left I called the number on the poster.

'Hello, bhai sahib, you need a room partner?' I asked.

The man on the other end asked me to speak in English. I thought he must be a very educated person as he spoke only in English and felt excited. After a day of being robbed and exploited, I had finally stumbled on to a good deal. In my broken English I fixed up a meeting with him at his room in the next fifteen minutes.

His room was not at all what I had expected. There were a few books, a table, a single chair and a mattress. That's it. There was a map of India on a wall. The kitchen was empty. There was a toilet but for bathing there was a tap outside.

I figured my future roommate spoke in English not because he was from another social class but because he didn't know any Hindi. He was from Kerala. Sharing the rent with him meant I had to pay him one thousand six hundred rupees a month. This included the electricity bill. I was happy with this arrangement and said yes.

Returning from Nehru Vihar to Dwarka that night, I was very pleased with myself. I thought I must be the first person in Delhi who had got a room for himself without a property dealer. Later I came to know that this was not entirely true but I spent my first night in the capital feeling that I had begun to master it. They say there is no knowledge greater than experience. In Delhi, I was gaining this knowledge.

19

Two weeks into our room-sharing, my roommate told me he had to leave. This was a big blow. I now had to either quickly find a partner or pay the entire rent myself. The latter was impossible. I had changed my initial plans about financing myself through tuitions.

My elder brother, who was in Assam, had generously agreed to finance my first year so I could focus on my studies, and hence I was especially careful about my money. Being new to the city, finding a new roommate was not simple either. But I had no other option. I too decided to make a few posters. Then I waited for the phone to ring.

Five days passed but there was no call. I could barely concentrate on my studies. One day it struck me that perhaps someone had put another poster over mine and I decided to go out and check. My poster hadn't been covered but someone had cleverly made my advertisement his own, replacing his phone number with mine. No wonder my phone was not ringing!

Around this time, I met an old friend from Patna. I was thrilled to see a familiar face, and so was he. He told me he too had come to Delhi to prepare for the UPSC exam but he was now working for HDFC Bank.

As I heard his story, I had a sudden, bleak, vision of my future. Young men and women take flight from smaller towns with the UPSC exam in their sights but end up at a workstation in some bank. This wasn't the life I wanted but would I too be forced to follow such a path? I pushed the thought away. As it is I was having problems finding a roommate. If I were to think too much about the uncertain future, my present would plunge into darkness.

Luckily, my friend told me of a room in the A block of the colony – my room was in the D block – and suggested I should shift there immediately. And thus I discovered yet another unspoken rule of Delhi life.

In the alphabet there may be no difference between A and D but in real life there is a huge discrimination between the two letters. Most of those living in the A block were financially comfortable while the D block mostly had labour-class residents. The atmosphere too was completely different. The D block was full of noise and hectic activity; only those who had no other options available to them lived there.

As soon as I moved into the room in the more upscale block I put up a poster advertising for a roommate. The very next day I got a call.

The person on the line was from Uttar Pradesh. His name was Piyush and his father was well placed in the state government. An alumnus of Hansraj College, the well-known Delhi University institution, he was smart and polite. When he came to meet me, I could tell he was an urban product and the city was not new to him.

The matter was settled and he moved in soon. When he brought his belongings in I could see he was well-off and also organized. To my eyes, it seemed as if he had everything required for living in Delhi – appliances for heating and cooling water, a large shelf, books in English.

Piyush's arrival brought peace into my life. I had no kitchen items and eating out was proving to be expensive. I suggested cooking ourselves but Piyush knew no cooking. He said we should hire a cook and he would pay, and I could reimburse him when my brother sent me money. We also fixed up with a woman to wash our clothes.

It was as though a perpetually drought-hit place had finally received rain. My roommate was not just my roommate, he was a big support for me.

He too was happy living with me. I didn't interfere in his affairs, nor did I ask him unnecessary questions. Where he went, whom he invited over to the room – I had nothing to do with all this. When his girlfriend was to come visiting, he would inform me well in advance. The understanding was that I should make myself scarce. I had no problem with this.

Our routines didn't match at all. When I was awake, he was asleep. He did nothing to keep the room clean. I was used to doing this myself since my Patna days and continued the practice here. It seemed a fair exchange for all his help. One day, as I was cleaning the room, I learnt of his caste. His certificates were lying outside. I happened to look at them and came to know he was a Dalit.

The assumptions I'd had about caste were shattered by this discovery. Piyush was so much richer and more sophisticated than me. His English too was far better than mine. I was beholden to him for his generosity and large-heartedness – he would even help me with money sometimes. Looking at him, no one could say he was a Dalit. Relationships are formed on the basis of life's requirements. I needed him as he did me and each of us was doing what we were expected to do by way of maintaining healthy social relations.

Those early months in Delhi were full of such lessons. Everybody talks about the big opportunities one can find in big cities. But nobody tells you about the great challenges that are very much part of life there.

Here in Delhi I was living in a social milieu that was

more diverse than anything I had ever seen. There was a lot more inequality and disparity among people. This made it difficult to form and maintain relations.

I tried to adopt the ways of this city. My way of dressing, my way of speaking – everything was going through a change. I could not be careless about what I wore any more. I made sure my clothes were properly cleaned and ironed and well fitting, aware that my appearance was being watched and judged.

My way of speaking – what many call the 'Bihari accent'– also underwent a transformation. Biharis speak Hindi mixed with one of the state's local languages, such as Maithili or Bhojpuri. In this mixed dialect, our Hindi is enriched with emotions and feelings and flavoured with unusual words. But to avoid being ridiculed or humiliated, I worked hard to ensure my Hindi was shorn of any provincial influence. I had to be careful not to sit on the floor of the Metro trains, something I'd have done instinctively, not to speak or laugh too loudly.

But the newness of city life brought about small joys too, with the discovery of an unknown street or alley seeming to open the door to another world. The early days in a big city usually contain adventure, curiosity, pleasure and pain. When you become used to the city, the pleasure and the pain both wane.

20

In Delhi I was determined to stay away from active politics. I wanted to focus on my studies and clear the UPSC exam. But two incidents pulled me back into the AISF within six months of my coming to the city.

Janchetna Prakashan, a leftist publication, had a mobile van which drove around the city selling books. On 10 January 2010, the van was parked close to the Arts Faculty in DU when activists belonging to the ABVP (Akhil Bharatiya Vidyarthi Parishad, the RSS's student wing) attacked it, vandalized it and beat up the people in it. In response, the Arts Faculty organized a protest rally near the Vivekananda statue, a popular site for protests at DU.

I took part in this rally. The incident had angered me – I wondered how students could attack a van that sold books. Many student organizations and social activists attended the rally. The ABVP attacked the protesters as well. It was a different kind of protest from the ones I was used to in Patna – more artistic, more sophisticated. In Patna we raised slogans with a matter-of-factness. The idea was to convey simple information but with passion and anger. Here in Delhi, it was different. The slogans were rich in imagination and were meant to be catchy, like songs. There was passion and anger too, but you cared about impressing your audience as much as informing them.

The people who gathered at this demonstration were also different. They seemed to belong to well-to-do families. Their clothes were better. The discussions at the meeting were intellectually of a higher level, too rich for the common man, who probably couldn't understand what was being said. But overall the proceedings impressed me because I could see the growing threat of the right wing and the crowd's need to be united against it. That day I returned to my room feeling satisfied.

The second incident happened ten days later in Nehru Vihar, near my neighbourhood. Nehru Vihar has a large population of Biharis, mostly vegetable sellers, daily wagers and students. Several of the landlords were also from Bihar. There was a clear divide between the locals and the migrant Bihari population, with constant tension between the two groups. For the locals, Ramlila and Devi ka Jagran were the two big events celebrated in the area. The migrant Biharis had their own celebrations depending on their professions. Bihari labourers performed the Vishwakarma puja while students did the Saraswati puja.

During the Saraswati puja, there was a quarrel between the local boys and the students. The local boys had a lot of free time – their families owned properties and they generally loafed around or played cricket in the park. The trouble on this occasion started with a minor scuffle between some boys but soon escalated. A random student was accosted on the road and beaten up for being a Bihari. The atmosphere became tense; everyone felt insecure. The students remained in hiding in their rooms.

I felt it was important to intervene. But I knew it would be impossible to stop a crowd of angry young men on my own. That required organized effort and connections. So I rang up an associate in the AISF. He was studying at the Law Faculty, DU. I had met him at one of the monthly meetings of the AISF study circle I had been attending casually. The AISF had no active organization in Delhi, just a handful of students like me who stayed in touch with the office. The study circle too was a small affair. But the office did have its contacts with politicians and intellectuals. I thought we should ask a political leader to help us.

We ended up going to the police and the problem was soon resolved. But it had unlocked something in me. It had been my first attempt to intervene in a real situation. Determined to study, I had earlier kept away from such issues but making a small difference had filled me with confidence. I thought that if simply being in touch with a political circle could help resolve such a grave situation, I could do even greater things as an activist.

The conflict also revealed to me the political layers of Nehru Vihar. Migrant labour and students had helped this locality to prosper. The wealthy class of Delhi did not care for this area but it had nonetheless become important because of its proximity to DU. Thanks to the large student population, coaching centres thrived here, as did businesses catering to them.

Ironically, the first generation of settlers in this colony had been immigrants themselves – refugees from Pakistan. But those roots had been erased and new-found wealth had made the original inhabitants arrogant. On the other hand, the migrant students were acutely aware that the local economy was dependent on them. They couldn't tolerate being addressed as Biharis in a derogatory manner. These complexities had led to tension then, and they still do.

These two incidents were of different kinds. The first was like an organized riot – as was the massacre in Gujarat in 2002 – while the second was the spontaneous reaction of a mob in response to the issue of identity – similar to what has been happening in Mumbai. Both were microcosms of incidents playing out all over the country.

The lesson I learnt from them was that I couldn't use my studies as an excuse to shy away from activism. If I saw someone being bullied I couldn't ignore it.

People get used to living with injustice; they keep getting treated badly and don't make any noise. It appeared that there were only two options – to bully or be bullied. I decided to be neither. I made up my mind to be a fighter, instead of becoming a bully or being bullied.

I remembered what Vishwajeet, the AISF leader in Patna, had said in my initial days with the student organization – fight to study, study to bring change. I felt that no matter where I was and what I did, I must be associated with the AISF and help build an active unit of the AISF in the city.

I began to attend the study circle regularly. It met once a month on a Saturday. At each meeting, a member would read his paper and there would be a discussion around it. At one meeting, the well-known economist Pritam Singh had come from London to read his paper on the Indian economy. I responded well to the discussion, asking many questions, and was asked to write a paper on unemployment.

My paper was well received. In my argument, I had moved slightly away from classical Marxism. Marx had not considered a growing population as a problem. For him the cause of poverty was the concentration of wealth. But I argued that if our population continued to increase at the current rate, we were heading for complete disaster.

S.N. Malakar, a professor at Jawaharlal Nehru University (JNU), was present at the meeting. This was the first time I was coming across someone from the famous university. I had never been to its campus. My friends in DU often hung out at the JNU campus and would invite me to come along but I always refused. I tended to stay in my room and study, determined not to stray from my target – the UPSC. I wanted to give the exam one genuine try.

Malakar sir disagreed with me at the study circle. He argued that it was inequality and capitalist greed that was the reason for poverty, not population. But I stuck to my guns. Neither of us won the debate but I came out feeling enlivened by the exchange of ideas. I rarely met or got to interact with someone of Professor Malakar's or Pritam Singh's stature. It was the first time I had debated with people of such repute and I had not been patronized or intimidated. They may have disagreed with me intensely but they treated me as an equal.

That year, I campaigned for the AISF candidates contesting in the students' union elections at DU. In Delhi, I saw a new aspect of student politics. Organizations like the ABVP and the NSUI (the National Students' Union of India, the Congress party's student wing) were openly distributing liquor and money to buy votes. Political parties were directly involved in the DU elections. Manoj Tiwari, the popular Bhojpuri singer, was roped in to woo Bihari voters while the NSUI arranged for film stars to perform.

The luring and seduction of voters is rampant in the country, be it student politics or politics at large. This kind of politics is harmful for voters – celebrities are used to lure people to vote for a particular party but these faces are like using a goat as bait to hunt down a lion.

In Patna we had fought for students' rights but such politics was nowhere to be seen here. In such an environment an organization like the AISF with its limited resources and principled stand found it difficult to compete. Despite these odds, one of our candidates won.

My contacts in the communist world of Delhi were increasing. I was in touch with political thinkers and writers like Anil Rajimwale and Krishna Jha, arguing with them about Marxism, the fall of the USSR and the failure of the Indian communist parties. I was beginning to make a place for myself in the AISF and gradually moving towards active politics.

21

Delhi was being decked up. It was the venue of the Commonwealth Games. Many young men from Nehru Vihar were among the volunteers – not to serve the nation but to get T-shirts, trousers and shoes.

The country took to talking obsessively about the massive preparations under way and the great costs around it. There were heroes and there were villains in the story. All the beggars in Delhi were rounded up and dumped into an open ground in Noida. Huge screens were put up around slums to camouflage them. Delhi was being decorated by covering up the ugly face of inequality. It seemed the government was not worried about poverty but about how to hide it from the world.

A hundred years ago, Delhi had been similarly dressed up when George V was to visit India in 1911. His royal procession was to start at Red Fort, wind its way through parts of Delhi (now Old Delhi) and reach the royal court.

Then too slums were covered behind huge sheets to hide them from the king's gaze. History was repeating itself. The only difference was that the country was now free, and instead of cloth, computer-designed flex curtains were used.

In the midst of this, my dreams of taking the UPSC exam were dealt a final blow. All these months, I had been preparing for the exams and had not taken any exam till date and now, in October 2010, the syllabus was changed. I was at my wits' end. To prepare for the new syllabus meant taking new coaching classes and starting from scratch. This was not possible. I needed another lakh to start preparing afresh. In addition, my older brother had got married and I couldn't pile my expenses on him.

It wasn't just my dreams that had been crushed. The UPSC stomps on countless such dreams every year. Hundreds of aspirants come to Delhi from all over the country with the dream of becoming someone. They live on a very tight budget, spending carefully from their parents' hard-earned money. They eat little, walk everywhere and wear the same clothes over and over again.

Every year, there are three lakh such aspirants for the precious one thousand seats. Those who get through are heroes; those who can't make it get lost in the crowd. While living in Nehru Vihar, I came across an army of such disillusioned youth. I saw how successive failures had turned them towards prostitution and drugs. Sometimes this would affect people in unexpected ways.

I knew one such person quite closely. He used to make all the arrangements for the 15 August and 26 January functions in the area. He invited me for one such function and that's how we got to know each other. He had come to the city to take the UPSC exam. The years passed, exams were held and the results announced. He was always unsuccessful.

Slowly, he started turning religious. To start with, he put up a picture of a god in his room. Gradually, the number of pictures increased. His room became filled with incense smoke. The 15 August and 26 January functions were forgotten and he became a sadhu, reading people's palms and doling out lucky charms.

In the meantime, I passed the MA course I had begun in Patna, but with only a second division. I had felt dissatisfied by the Nalanda Open University experience – there was no question that distance learning kept you at a distance from learning. Despite my unimpressive results, I realized that I wanted to be an academic. It was the only profession that would suit my interest in ideas and learning, and let me pursue my political dreams.

I felt that academics is a better place where one can earn decently while still living a conscious life. For the first time, I could not see a contradiction between my mental satisfaction and material condition.

At the AISF study circle I spoke to Malakar sir. He suggested that I apply for an MPhil degree in JNU. I bought a form in Nehru Vihar, filled it up and took the test. Shortly, I got to know that I had cleared my written exams.

I had applied to two centres at the School of International Studies – Russian studies and African studies. I didn't know anyone at the university other than Malakar sir. Since he was a professor in African studies, I had put that down as my first choice and so I was selected for that. I wished I had put down the Russian centre instead so I could have studied Marxism and Leninism in greater detail. But my choice had been made. African studies it was to be. And this was how I got into JNU.

It was a decision that was to completely change my life.

Part 4

JNU

22

You can never forget your first encounter with JNU.

But I have to admit I felt a twinge of disappointment on my first visit, standing at the main entrance – the North Gate. It looked so ordinary. You couldn't tell a prestigious university lay beyond those gates.

I had to go to Brahmaputra Hostel. Some friends of friends lived there and I needed their help to prepare for my vivas. The guard at the gate told me that the hostel was located furthest from the entrance and advised me to take a bus. But I decided to walk instead.

The distance between North Gate and Brahmaputra Hostel is a mere two kilometres. But I had no idea then that it was going to be the most important journey of my life. With every step I took I would be leaving my earlier life far behind.

The disappointment I had felt as I entered the gates

vanished as I walked. I couldn't believe this was Delhi. It was the monsoon and the scene around me was lush and green with hills in the distance. I've always loved the mountains. With winding paths, neelgai and peacocks, this was truly an enchanting place. It felt like another world altogether.

That day I had another unique experience. A person riding a bike was hit by a bus. There was no serious damage but a crowd of students collected around the accident site. Soon they were divided into two groups. One group was upset with the bus driver's careless driving inside the campus. They wanted to thrash him. The other group disagreed. They felt that if the driver was at fault he should be handed over to the police.

This was unbelievable. What kind of a university was this where students were talking of letting the law take its own course? So far I had only seen brute force being used on such occasions – in Patna a fight was sure to break out during such incidents. But here, minds were being applied.

That night I stayed on campus. The student I had come to meet didn't have place for me in his room but he sent me to another hostel – Jhelum – to spend the night. I loved the atmosphere in the hostels. All of them had a great collection of books and there were mattresses strewn around, with three to four men sleeping side by side. The hostels were either girls only or boys only or had separate wings for girls and boys; girls came and went freely to boys' rooms. This phenomenon, which I initially found odd, later started to seem natural, correct and beautiful.

It was the viva season and the place was full of candidates who had come to stay with friends to prepare for the test. And so the number of students on campus was far more than the number to whom rooms were allotted. One look at the hostels and you could tell that this was not home just for those who were from the university. Anyone who needed a place to stay in Delhi and prepare for admission in JNU could find shelter here. I felt that I was in a university for the first time. This is how all centres of learning should be, I thought to myself.

Finding your way in JNU as a newbie is like trying to find your way in a maze. As I wandered, dazed, from the eating mess to Jhelum, I didn't mind getting lost. Something else surprised me. It was 2 a.m. And girls were walking on the campus streets on their own. There were so many forests and hills; how could it be safe for girls to be alone in such an environment?

Somehow I managed to go to sleep. But soon I was up again – there was an aircraft flying above the hostel and its noise woke me up. I asked my host how he could sleep through all the noise. He said, 'Prepare well for the interview and you'll get the answer', and went back to sleep.

On the day of the viva, I came well prepared. I found the appearance of some of the candidates odd. They didn't look as if they had come for an interview. There seemed to be two kinds of applicants. One lot, like me, who had arrived in borrowed belts and shoes, and the other lot, with a jhola hanging over their shoulder, who seemed not to bother at all about how they looked – whether they wore shoes or chappals, whether they had shaved or not.

I walked into the interview room nervously. The faculty's attitude put me completely at ease. The first question they asked was whether I'd like to speak in Hindi or English. I said Hindi and was asked all the questions in my mother tongue.

The results were announced and I discovered to my great joy that I had been selected for my MPhil. I gave up the room in Nehru Vihar and moved to JNU carrying only one bag. I was allotted a room in Sutlej Hostel, right next to Jhelum. For me, who had come from a village, lived in the city briefly and finally reached JNU, a new chapter was unfolding.

Everything felt fresh and new. For instance, there was no discrimination between seniors and juniors. Brahmaputra is considered JNU's senior-most hostel, as it houses only PhD scholars in their later years. But everyone there treated me as an equal and I didn't for a moment feel that I was a fresher.

One day I got over-involved during a discussion, and found myself arguing vehemently. At one point I felt I was talking too much. I said to a senior, self-consciously, that I had probably spoken too much and that he should forgive me if I had caused offence. He replied, 'Don't embarrass me by asking for forgiveness.' No one coming from the feudal set-up of Bihar could have expected a response like this.

Living on campus was a culture shock. The atmosphere was free. Boys and girls walked about together late into the night. In colleges in Bihar, boys and girls had to look for places to be together. There was hardly anywhere they could sit in privacy. And if they were caught doing so they could be punished. In JNU there were no such restrictions.

Women were not just more confident on campus but were also very conscious of their rights. Whether it was to do with sloganeering, helping new students with the admission process or recruiting people to one's political organization, they had complete equality in all activities. Girls were present in equal numbers to boys – in classrooms, in protests, at the dhaba. In fact, sometimes they outnumbered men. In my class I was the only man, the remaining nine were girls.

The classroom didn't feel like a classroom at all. With its round table, it felt more like a conference room. On my first day, I stood up when the teacher entered, as was my habit. He asked me, 'Why are you standing? Is this a school?' I said, 'Of course it's a school. School of International Studies.'

He laughed at my response and asked me to sit down. Even the faculty was different. Instead of being aloof as most teachers were, they were friendly with the students and preferred to talk to them as equals. I quickly discovered that I could challenge any professor and disagree with him or her. Our discussions were always held on equal terms. And in our own language too.

Every day I seemed to learn something new; every day I discovered something astonishing in that early period. I hadn't ever been exposed to people from different cultures and places before JNU. Now I was encountering them from all over the country and indeed the world. Of my two initial roommates at Sutlej, one was Bihari, the other Rajasthani. I got along with my Rajasthani roommate much better. This was the first time I had a good friend who was not from Bihar. To see people from all over the world you usually have to go to different countries. In JNU you'll find them without having to step outside the campus. Here it is easy for the common man to enter, but for VIPs it is difficult. The special treatment that they desire is not laid out for them.

The JNU guard's job is not just to keep outsiders away, it is also to help them. Of course he will chase away troublemakers but then not everybody falls in that category. So why view everyone with suspicion? In our society being poor is equivalent to being a criminal. If you're poor it is assumed you're in the category of thieves and thugs, whereas the fact is that poverty is created by the corruption of a few. A man becomes poor when he's deprived of the fruits of his hard work. To then view him as a criminal is the case of the pot calling the kettle black.

All that I saw changed the way I viewed the world and shaped my politics. For instance, one's first response on seeing the Taj Mahal is to admire its magnificence. We are humbled and awed by its beauty and grandeur. But if you visit the Taj Mahal after JNU you will think of it as a monument built out of the sweat and toil of ordinary, oppressed people like you and me.

I learnt in JNU that it is not essential to be proficient in English to be in politics. Spotless white clothes are not required. Having money is not a must. Sometimes the backing of a large organization is not essential. If you come from a poor or deprived background and talk about it, your voice is more effective than that of someone who owns a car or wears fancy clothes. In JNU, if someone is not really poor but indulges in politics for the poor, nobody will believe him.

Throughout the world the people who walk on footpaths – the downtrodden – are those on the margins of politics, but the same people lead politics in JNU. They have also been able to literally save the footpaths. The downtrodden may not have a roof above their heads and may have to make the footpath their home but in JNU they become thinkers and leaders.

The world outside JNU works the other way around. There the belief is that someone who is himself needy cannot do much for others. And so the display of power becomes important. But within JNU, power lies with those on the side of truth and those who give it its rightful due.

Politics takes place everywhere. In classrooms, in dormitories, in meetings and above all over long chats in the dhabas. This is the true home of chai and charcha. The most legendary of the dhabas is Ganga dhaba. I once heard a song about JNU. It said 'Forget McD and CCD, come let's go to Ganga dhaba'. Here discussion is more important than tea, company more important than food. And the company and tea you can find at Ganga dhaba are hard to find anywhere else.

I took to spending most of my evenings there. In the 2014 elections, Modiji was also doing chai pe charcha and talking of how to sell the people of the nation over tea in a dhaba. Now when the administration attempts to close down the JNU dhabas, it is actually trying to end the debate–discussion culture of the university. It is afraid of the culture of openness and questioning that flourishes here.

22

After giving up on the UPSC I had decided to be an activist. But I had always been torn between joining politics and concentrating on doing well in my exams and securing my future. In JNU I found a platform where I could be politically active while studying. The posters on the walls pulled me towards them and I allowed myself to be pulled.

My political involvement with JNU started very early, even before I was formally admitted to the university. JNU follows a unique practice of admission assistance. Student organizations set up help desks near the administrative block and assist applicants in filling out the lengthy forms and verifications required by different offices.

I come from a place where even the sight of a huge building or its gate inspires fear. People from back home would not even dare enter such a place. And if they were faced with sheets of forms to fill, they would run a mile.

Most students coming to JNU are from similar social and economic backgrounds. Considering this, to have senior students and workers taking you through the forms is extremely welcome.

But there is also an underlying agenda – the help desks are set up by political parties as a way to attract the new students. Each comes with its own coloured flag. I walked towards the AISF's red flag and began to make myself useful to the other members. And so even before my admission I had started becoming involved.

Going by the size of the tents and tables, it was not difficult to see which one belonged to the ruling parties. None of the help desks had a shade over them, except two – the BJP and the Congress student bodies, the ABVP and the NSUI. The irony was that even though their tables were the fanciest, there was hardly anyone there. The real competition here was between the left parties.

You'll be reading this and laughing, no doubt. Utopia doesn't exist, you are probably thinking, and it's true that in my first few months I was dazzled by my new university. But as I became more politically active I discovered cracks in the perfect facade.

For instance, casteism outside JNU is visible, casteism inside JNU is not. But it exists. It's not essential that the man who shouts slogans the loudest follows that particular philosophy in real life. The man who says

'Brahminvaad murdabad' (death to Brahminism) could be a hardcore Brahminist.

While contesting elections I saw an ugly side of JNU. Caste was an important criterion while selecting a candidate. Representation had to be there from all centres (departments) and with students of different castes. I thought it unfair on principle.

Despite its flaws, the scope for protest was infinite in JNU. It could be a hostel-related issue, like disrupted water supply or a fellowship not coming through on time, a social–cultural standpoint or a matter of international politics such as Israel attacking Palestine – there were processions, speeches and meetings. When I was new and was not sectarian I attended all these meetings, including ABVP's, and was vocal in all of them.

My habit of asking questions started in the classroom. India was beginning to increase its initiatives in Africa and an attempt was being made from both sides to strengthen relations among the countries. In my broken English I asked if Africa was once again being colonized. Britain and other European countries had once looted Africa in the nineteenth century – was India now joining that list? Were relations between the people of Africa and the people of India truly improving? Or was the ground being prepared for Indian businesses to flourish in those markets?

All eyes turned to me as I asked these questions. By now, outside the classroom I had been branded as a leftist. Inside the classroom, this was my first branding. On leaving the room I was immediately asked – are you a Marxist? I answered that I didn't know, I was simply asking something that had been on my mind.

People very quickly branded you at JNU. No one directly asked you your caste or politics. But discreet inquiries were made and, very soon, opinions were formed. You are the organization you belong to, without the right to have your own point of view. And conversely, whether your organization has taken the right stand or wrong, you are expected to support it.

At an ABVP meeting, a person looking like a sadhu was speaking on spirituality. He said that we reap the fruit of our karma and our next life is determined on its basis. I asked him, when Brahma first created the world how did he determine lifeforms? After all, no one had a past record of karma then.

Instead of answering me he began to speak of my Hindi, how good it was, and how articulate I was. He had no answer to my comment and didn't attempt to address my question. Eventually I came to the conclusion that in ABVP meetings it's no point asking anyone anything. No one expects you to question your party. Despite all the drawbacks of leftist meetings – above all how quickly you were judged by what party you belonged to – what I liked about them was that you are allowed to ask questions, even if you may not always like the answers.

On a long walk, it's much more exciting to take an unknown route, to lose one's way and finally reach the top. Taking the well-trodden path is boring and unexciting. Politics for me was somewhat like this – especially in my first few months at university. I was trying this and trying that. Enthusiastically asking questions. Throwing myself into everything.

I don't like it when some say I lost my way and so ended up in politics. Actually, I explored many paths and chose politics. I got pushed around in life and, bruised and battered, ended up in politics. Those who are being roughed up in life must enter politics. There is no other option. As Premchand said, if you haven't experienced the summer heat you can't enjoy the first raindrops of monsoon. Someone who has experienced no pain in life doesn't have the desire to be free of it. Even if his life has no discomfort he doesn't realize it. He who has not experienced hunger doesn't value food. You run after flavour only when your belly is somewhat full.

When I joined JNU I was not shooed away or made to feel like I was intruding, as it usually happens with the poor. When a poor man enters the Metro or a mall he can sense people's disgust. And this destroys his self-confidence. In complete contrast to this is the ordinary entrance gate of JNU, which beckons one and all, welcoming each one, saying this place is for you. This gives a huge boost to one's self-confidence.

All places have their own sloganeering culture. So does JNU. It was here for the first time that I saw the dafli or drums being played as slogans were shouted. The slogans were also set to a tune and sung. I too learnt to play the dafli.

In the village if you are caught fooling around with an instrument, the ustad will scold you as though a major misstep has occurred. This used to happen a lot during my IPTA days in my village. I once said to the ustad, after making yet another mistake, that he too must have been a beginner once, prone to errors. He replied that he too had learnt by being scolded by his ustad.

None of us knows anything at birth. One has to learn everything. And what is required for this is opportunity and encouragement. Arjun had the opportunity so he became an ace archer. But when Eklavya learnt on his own through perseverance and hard work, his thumb was chopped off. There is no such thing as merit. Opportunity is supreme. And JNU provides this to all.

The world outside JNU couldn't be more different. You constantly get pushed around when you try to learn anything. In JNU you are given the space to make mistakes and learn. It's how all universities should be. Initially I used to be part of the crowd and shyly listen to speeches and sloganeering. Then I couldn't stop myself and began to cheer from the crowd. Then a day came when I myself wanted to shout slogans. I too wanted to say – Inquilab zindabad.

Even if you're new at JNU, others will fall silent and allow you to have your say. Elsewhere, usually if you start with your slogan either no one will follow or someone else will outshout you. Here people let you speak. Your tone may not be perfect, your pitch may not be right, but nobody will mock you for it. Instead you will be supported and encouraged, so you can pick up things.

I had been taking part in debates since I was in school. But the debates there followed a set pattern. Our aim in those events was to win awards and competitions. But in JNU, we focused on winning over the students and bringing them round to our point of view. We'd often end up having detailed and heated arguments on national and international politics and rural issues in faraway villages. The real challenge was to remain consistent about one's ideas even after the debate. This was how one could acquire the students' trust. It wasn't just about making a clever point for its own sake.

It took me a while to understand this. I observed all the speakers carefully, the how, when and what of what they spoke. Gradually I picked up the nuances of public speaking. But I didn't imitate anybody's style.

I decided to focus on the ideas and arguments in my speech. And what I wanted to say would be determined by the way I saw the world. As for style, I decided to speak in a language which was easy for anyone to understand.

People often ask me about my speeches. It might surprise you to know that I never write my speeches and no one writes them for me either. They arise instead from my conversations with people – each conversation and argument adding a layer to my thinking, sharpening some ideas, forcing me to discard others. I try to talk to people everywhere, learn more about their thinking, what their concerns are and how they express them.

So you can say that my speeches are an extension of my conversations – that's why Ganga dhaba was so important for me! I try to weave everyday examples and imagery with the points I am making. So whenever my audience faces a real-life issue, rising prices for example, they also remember the politics behind it. The message then becomes ingrained in their hearts. I never make up anything. I see myself as a mirror, as the reflection of the people, taking up their concerns, adding the bigger political picture to it and reflecting it back to them through my speeches.

Once I had to address the JNU security guards. The security guards are employed through a private security agency in JNU and most of them are underpaid and overworked and since there is no job security they are unable to fight for their rights in a unified voice. I had to convince them to fight for their rights and speak to the JNU administration for minimum wages rather than depend on the private agency to address their grievances. To help them understand their situation I told them a story. If they got a job, I said, with a sethji using the help of someone they knew, would they go to the sethji with their problems or the acquaintance who helped them get that job? The acquaintance is nothing more than a middleman. You had to make demands to the one you worked for. It made it simple for the guards to see the logic in this and relate it back to their own situation.

If the audience cannot understand what you are saying about their lives, your speech becomes meaningless. I try to make my arguments in an easy and relatable manner so I use incidents and stories. I also try to use poetry. Though I haven't been an especially serious student of poetry, I have managed to learn some beautiful verses and I use them whenever I can.

My first speech in JNU was in March 2012 when I contested for the position of councillor of my centre. At the time there were no students' unions. The 2006 Lyngdoh Committee set up to frame guidelines for students' union elections had aimed to curb money and muscle power in the students' unions. It recommended an age limit for contestants and said that a student could fight only once for the post of office-bearers. It gave the university or college administration the right to cancel the candidature of any student.

These recommendations had major implications. If implemented, they would curb the political life of a campus and the growth and evolution of student leaders who honed their skills through years of campaigning and becoming a part of the student political body. Also the union would become dependent on the very administration it had to fight with for students' rights!

Naturally the recommendations were rejected by the JNU students' union. And the Supreme Court ordered a stay on JNUSU elections in October 2008. In accordance with the students' union constitution, the elected union was given an extension of its terms by the University General Body Meeting (UGBM) and it kept running things. But this came to a halt in 2010 when the entire union leadership handed its resignation. Since then there had been no students' union.

Finally, in January 2012, JNU students decided that elections would be held, after making some exceptions to the Lyngdoh Committee recommendations. The Supreme Court lifted the stay on JNUSU elections and the students set the date for elections in March 2012.

The campus was gripped by a new kind of fever – we were seeing an election after more than three years. You could feel the excitement in the air – the upcoming elections became the sole topic of conversation in the hostels, canteens and dhabas.

Students felt that they would now have a union which would take up their demands and fight for their rights. There was also a great deal of curiosity about who would fight the elections. Some of the established student leaders began to interact with other students with more warmth and charm, starting their courtship of the electorate early. This change in atmosphere both confused and amused me.

At an AISF meeting we decided to form a coalition with the Students' Federation of India (SFI), a student organization associated with the Communist Party of India (Marxist).

Quite often when I told people that I worked for the AISF, they would respond with a curious question – which organization is this? It took me by surprise that in a politically active campus like JNU people didn't know the country's oldest student body, one which had even taken part in the freedom movement. Then I realized this was not lack of information, it was a clever way of not acknowledging our presence, of putting us down.

The coalition was formed. The left parties united. We had two major opponents: the communal-minded ABVP and the opportunist All-India Students' Association (AISA), the student wing of CPI (M-L) Liberation, that had been leading JNUSU for the past several years. The latter was also a left organization but we were uniting against it. What kind of unity was this? We intended to unite all the left forces against the right wing and ended up uniting against an organization which belonged to the left.

The AISF was rather small as was the membership. So I was asked to contest even though I was only in my first year. I had never fought an election. In Patna we fought to hold elections and I had moved from Patna to Delhi chanting this demand. But truth be told, I had never seen one play out. And now when I was going to see an election for the first time I was being asked to contest in it as well. I tried my best to get out of it. I said my English was poor, coursework was on, that my studies would suffer. But eventually I had to give in.

My lack of electoral experience became obvious during canvassing. I'd introduce myself to people, and forget to ask for their vote. I was new to JNU and so whenever I went to the students' hostel rooms to ask for votes, I would end up being distracted by the books kept there, the posters stuck on the walls. My campaign in-charge had to remind me to introduce myself. I would do so and then clam up again.

Students would ask me why I had come. I am fighting elections, I would answer. So why have you come to us if you are fighting elections, they would respond mockingly. I would say shyly, to ask for votes. They would then laugh and say, then ask for a vote, why are you standing so quietly?

I was full of nerves. I hesitated to speak while distributing my pamphlet, not introducing myself unless my campaign in-charge nudged me to do so. I found it very difficult to approach people I didn't know. It was excruciating. I felt embarrassed and mortified that I had to push myself in this way.

There was only one saving grace. I had never had trouble speaking in public – it seemed to require different skills from a face-to-face interaction – and so it was proved again. My first speech was at the general body meeting (GBM) of all the students of a particular school. Prior to the voting, a GBM is held in every school, in which all the contestants for the council speak.

After my first speech many people came and told me, comrade, you spoke well. I had said that I wasn't fighting against AISA. I wasn't fighting in the election because I wanted to become a councillor or a part of the central panel. I was fighting so that we could defeat the ABVP. This was something even AISA members appreciated and so did the SFI. But from then on I became the target of the ABVP.

After coming to JNU I had observed the ABVP closely. ABVP members lived on the campus and made full use of the democratic space it provided but constantly badmouthed JNU as well as the very leftist and activist forces that had fought so hard for this democracy. While eating in the mess, the ABVP students would often make the point that JNU didn't rank among the top universities of the world.

I naively wondered why, if they hated JNU so much,

they didn't just leave and go somewhere else? Later I understood that they spoke this way because they felt sidelined here. Like everyone else they have the space and freedom to speak as they like, but no one here appreciates their views.

I feared that if such people gained political prominence JNU would be destroyed. That JNU, where the son or daughter of a Dalit, adivasi, backward class or minority can do PhD, that JNU will not survive. Our rights and our space will cease to exist. The JNU that will emerge will have an elaborate gate, a barrier will be put, the sight of which will intimidate a poor man, or any 'other'. On entering, show of force will start with the security guard himself who will scold the poor fellow. Seniors of the hostel will terrorize him, and creativity and original thought will no longer exist in the classroom. A particular kind of thinking will be imposed on everyone and, in the name of cleanliness and order, Brahminism. The free environment of the campus will disappear. The self-confidence that a poor, weak and common man gains by being in JNU will not be there for him any more.

(After the elections in 2012, the JNU students' union arranged for a band to play on Labour Day. The ABVP was very critical of the expense being incurred. Initially, I too felt this was a wasteful expenditure. Later we found out that no money had been spent on it. Members of the band were themselves activists and had performed without charging anything. However, the ABVP soon invited Manoj Tiwari to perform and I found this hypocritical. When they do it, it's a cultural evening, but when we do it, it's extravagance.)

They also seem to be against anyone who is from the weaker sections of society – women, Dalits, Muslims, backward classes, adivasis. They usually crowd around the hostel gate and pass offensive remarks when girls pass by or go inside with a boy. Their general refrain is that JNU has turned into an immoral, lawless place, students come here to have a good time, hostels have turned into family quarters, why should girls be allowed to use the toilets in the men's hostels, etc. The ABVP for example said that the toilets had run out of water because of girls using them. It was interesting that they never blamed the Jal Board for the water shortage.

Students and others living in Munirka often come to JNU for clean water. Not everyone can afford a fridge or a water filter. ABVP boys also blamed these people for using up the water. In my experience the ABVP members think of the world as 'us' and 'them'.

I could empathize with Munirka residents who couldn't afford a fridge. In them I could see both my past and my future. After completing my PhD, I knew I would not get a job. As I wouldn't be going to 'America', I'd be living in Munirka or a similar such place. Modiji can go to America but not every tea-seller can.

In my speech I decided to take them head on. I asked them, why do you have to fight here? Everything is yours anyway. If you want there can be a helipad in JNU. If you want there can even be a swimming pool. If you want each student can get not just a room but an entire flat. The audience enjoyed this and there was much applause.

Soon it was voting day. After the Lyngdoh Committee recommendations came into force, campaigning was reduced to ten days when earlier it had been a month. And so the campaign had taken place extra fast.

On the day of the voting I was so tired that I went off to sleep by early evening. I slept the whole night and all of the next day and woke up only in the evening. I was too afraid to ask anyone about the results and sat quietly outside the school building where the votes were being counted. Slowly people started gathering around me. They hugged me, reassured me and tried to boost my morale. Dazed, still exhausted, I understood that I had lost and they were sympathizing with me.

My organization lost badly. I, however, found the results satisfactory. The organization that had won was also from the left. I never viewed left unity as an election-time expediency. I believed and still do that all leftist parties must remain united on the ground at all times.

That same year the SFI broke up. In fact, it was in JNU that the SFI unit disintegrated. The issue was CPM's support of Pranab Mukherjee as the presidential candidate. The JNU unit of the SFI opposed this. They saw Mukherjee as pro-liberalization and a friend of big business, and couldn't accept the idea of CPM supporting him.

Student organizations may not accept that they are wings of various political parties, but in JNU everyone knows this is the case. Here they are necessarily viewed as subsets of political parties and so they are held accountable for larger political decisions. For instance, in JNU, the SFI had to answer a lot of questions related to the policies of the CPM government regarding the police violence in West Bengal's Nandigram and Singur villages. The unit eventually broke away due to differences on the issue of support to Mukherjee.

I've noticed that whenever communist parties have split in the country the reasons behind it have invariably been personal. The breaks are presented as an effect of irreconcilable ideological differences but the real reasons are to do with power politics within the party. This break-up was no different. In the leftist parties, we keep harping on democracy but when it comes to decision-making we ignore democratic principles.

The breakaway group started calling itself SFI-JNU. In

the next elections – held six months later, in September – AISF and this breakaway party formed a coalition. The next president of JNUSU, V. Lenin Kumar, came from this coalition. In this election I saw some other aspects of local politics; for instance, I learnt about the techniques of vote shift or vote transfer in which two or more organizations can for different posts distribute the vote of their cadre among different candidates. This is an unstated agreement but the cadre and a few loyal supporters are told about it although usually by the end the whole campus gets to know about it.

25

The country was in political turmoil. The ruling Congress party had been caught in a large number of high-profile scams. Anna Hazare's powerful anti-corruption movement was gathering momentum while the BJP and ABVP were on the rise in the distant horizon.

Several political parties and organizations were getting involved in the Anna Hazare movement. Many leftist organizations also supported it, choosing to ignore the fact that the RSS was deeply involved with it. Each and every organization within the Anna Hazare movement, overtly or covertly, supported the RSS philosophy. Some of these people went on to become ministers, governors and contenders for chief minister posts under the BJP-led central government. Arvind Kejriwal, one of the early prominent faces of the movement, eventually broke with Hazare partly on this issue.

I can imagine that similar circumstances must have

prevailed in the lead-up to the Emergency. It was wrong to impose Emergency, but it was preceded by an agitation orchestrated by the RSS. In fact, there is a poem by the famous Hindi and Maithili poet Baba Nagarjun, who was arrested during the Emergency, where he says that it was a mistake to participate in the agitation.

The Anna Hazare movement was going through its ups and downs when a violent incident of rape took place in Delhi on 16 December 2012. People in Delhi and the country rose in unison against this. There was widespread anger among people – there had been many rapes, but this brutal attack touched a chord among the middle class.

I was at an acquaintance's home on 17 December when I saw the news on television. We were on our winter break but some JNU students demonstrated at the police station. Slowly their numbers grew. Later, demonstrators were attacked by the police, which incited people even more. JNU played an important role in all this, leading much of the Delhi demonstrations and subsequently helping the Justice Verma committee with the rape law reforms.

Protesters blocked roads and a candlelight march to Safdarjung Hospital was announced, leading to other marches across different parts of the country. JNU students went to protest at India Gate and they managed to sneak into the home ministry, catching the police by surprise. Then another big protest was announced at North Block which houses the home ministry.

The police resorted to a lathi charge that day, and water cannons were used to disperse the protesters. But nothing could break the spirit of the protesters. The rape had captured the imagination of the entire nation, standing for something bigger than itself, reflecting some of the dissatisfactions of the country. The protesters assembled again the next day at the same spot. Once again they were put down by force.

For the first time I experienced the way the media can blow up an issue. The positive outcome was that the middle class came out and spoke up. To represent their political aspirations, a new party – the Aam Aadmi Party (AAP) under the leadership of the former Anna Hazare aide Arvind Kejriwal – came to life.

In the midst of this turmoil, the BJP was steadily gaining ground. There was no other party to give direction to the deep disappointment that was building up against the Congress. AAP did get attention but its presence was limited to only a few cities, and it had no national footprint at all. Stepping into this space and making optimum use of media and social media, the BJP moved ahead rapidly. Soon Gujarat's chief minister, Narendra Modi, was being talked about as the future prime minister.

The JNU campus was going through its own period

of turmoil, attacked on every front. This included a slow increase in fees and a reduction in the subsidy given by the government. The mess bills in the hostels were on the rise; the half-yearly registration fees for the hostels were increased. There was an acute shortage of hostels and students were forced to rent accommodation outside the campus. There was also no increase in scholarships. All this had an impact on the poorer students and their families.

Alongside this, we witnessed an increase in attacks on people's rights, which saw a corresponding increase in conversations around subalterns and their rights. Beef was banned from one of the canteens. Students who talked of eating beef and pork were targeted by the administration and the Sangh Parivar. In Narmada hostel, liquor was mixed in water coolers during the holy month of Ramzan.

This was the background in which the prominent left party in the campus, AISA, won the JNU elections in 2013. They used the issue of the hostels as their main campaign plank but never tried to address the underlying reasons for it. So the problem only festered during their tenure.

In May 2014, general elections were held in the country and the BJP swept to power in a massive landslide. Soon people realized there was a difference between the Congress and the BJP. Under the Congress, you could hold a major protest, as we had done to protest against the brutal rape in Delhi in December 2012. Under the new government even a small demonstration was not possible.

This became evident on the very day Narendra Modi was to take oath. In 2002, when Modi was still chief minister of the state, the Akshardham Mandir, a well-known temple in Gujarat, had been the site of a terrorist attack. Six people were arrested for the crime. Yet eleven years later, they were released on the grounds that the charges against them had been false. In the trial the Supreme Court criticized the Gujarat police for its shoddy investigation. The JNU students wanted to protest outside Gujarat Bhawan against the arrest of such innocent people, and for falsely implicating them and keeping them in prison without proof. Many of these men were young and had wasted precious years.

Even before the bus could leave JNU the police waylaid it. It was the first time we had seen them in the campus. That day five truckloads of cops entered the campus and informed us that we could not go anywhere. But because the number of students was so large they did not succeed. And so they hijacked the bus in which students were leaving. We were diverted from central Delhi near Safdarjung's Tomb and taken to Jantar Mantar, where the city's public protests take place.

At the time Akbar Choudhry was the president of the JNU student body. He asked me to be the first speaker at the Jantar Mantar gathering which was swarming with agitated students. Normally, because ours is a small organization, we are the last to be called in. But that day Akbar called me first as he felt I could speak to the police most effectively. They listened to my speech intently. Usually the cops do not listen to speeches in events like these, nor do they react to them. But that day many of them came up to me saying they agreed with me.

That day I got many messages suggesting we set up a new anti-fascist, anti-communal group. The AISF began to work towards this and we formed the Left Progressive Front (LPF). This included the Democratic Students' Federation (DSF, the new name for SFI-JNU), Students for Social Justice and students who were not associated with any organization but felt the need for a platform like this one. The slogan for this new front was 'Jai Bhim Lal Salaam'.

It was a slogan which wove together the legacy of two different movements. The Dalit Ambedkarites who fought for a casteless society had Jai Bhim as their slogan while Lal Salaam, a slogan of the communist movement, looked to build an egalitarian social order.

My teacher Professor Tulsiram used to say any movement fighting against the establishment and for equality – be it feminist, environmental, workers' or farmers' movements – cannot survive in isolation and will need to come together with other organizations. And that is why Jai Bhim and Lal Salaam came together.

This marked the beginning of new politics in JNU. Everyone felt the need to be united. But no contestant of the LPF won any central posts in the 2014 elections. What was worrying was that the vote share of the ABVP and their number of councillors went up as well.

Then Trilokpuri in East Delhi was struck by communal attacks.

There is a legacy JNU has inherited. Whenever anything happens in the country, oppression, injustice, struggle, all eyes turn to JNU with hope. And when any untoward incident happens in the neighbourhood, people look to JNU for help. For instance, across the JNU gate there is a tea shop. The owner's son disappeared and the owner came to JNU students for help. In a slum area near Vasant Kunj a girl got lost and the community came to JNU students for help. Earlier, JNU students had agitated for refugees from Myanmar – most of these were Rohingya Muslims who had got displaced from their homes.

So now when there was trouble in Trilokpuri, all student bodies, except the ABVP, went to the neighbourhood on a fact-finding mission. Trilokpuri is a decrepit area and like all localities inhabited by workers and poor people it is not easily accessible.

When we reached there, we saw that the bricks which had been hurled during the attacks had left their mark on the roads, making them red. The shops in the Muslim basti were burnt, their locks broken, and strewn all around were charred remains of the goods and furniture destroyed. The Muslims said that this was not the work of an unruly mob. It was a well-planned attack intended to terrorize Muslims and finish them off economically.

We then went to the Valmiki mohalla, where the lower castes live. There some people we met initially accused the Muslims of burning their own shops to make money out of insurance. But some Dalits in the area pointed to the role of the Sangh Parivar in this. They showed us a school there being run by the right-wing organization.

As I had discovered in Nehru Vihar, this area too had its share of tensions among the different communities, its own internal politics and rivalries. But this time the usual fight was given a communal colour. Every experience I had confirmed in my mind that if the oppressed and the downtrodden don't unite, this government would finish them off simply by making them fight with each other. It was essential that the weaker sections come together.

But even in JNU our experiment at unity didn't survive for long. In 2015 when the AISF proposed that we form a left progressive front to contest the elections together, the other left organizations rejected the idea. As a result, all leftist and Ambedkarites contested elections separately, votes got divided and the ABVP won a seat in the central panel.

There was, however, some good news on a personal front. In this election I had decided to contest as president on behalf of the AISF. I had taken part in a number of movements by now – my views had become stronger, I had gained in confidence. I felt I was ready to take on a larger role. This time around, the campaigning was very different and much less fraught. People now recognized me and I too had no hesitation in asking them for their vote.

The big presidential debate was held on the last day of campaigning. As usual I did not prepare from any book. Nor was I nervous. I had the experience of four years of activism, and I was able to put the essence of my thinking into a ten-minute speech linking up a number of issues and trying to put them in context.

The JNU presidential debate is attended by hundreds, sometimes thousands of students and it has a huge impact on the election results. You don't have to just put forth your stand but also answer your competitors' and the student body's questions. The debate shows a candidate's preparedness, his or her political understanding and his or her popularity.

One major concern of mine was the fast pace at which higher education was being privatized. At the same time the students' union was being weakened by the Lyngdoh Committee recommendations. I decided to begin my speech by speaking against those recommendations – many unions under AISA leadership had done nothing about it. I appealed to the students to vote against the Lyngdoh Committee recommendations on election day. My promise was that if I won the elections, the next elections would be under JNU student union constitution.

I reiterated my larger political vision. The need for left unity in the face of growing fascist attacks across the country. Elections were to be held in Bihar and the left was fighting it together, but in JNU the AISA refused to fight the elections with the other left organizations. AISA might not think this unity to be important, I said, but the people of the country would take to the streets to bring about this unity.

I also attacked the ABVP and RSS. A Muslim candidate was made to misquote from the Quran and give a hate speech. I strongly criticized this: just like the 56-inch chest is a lie, so is your rally, so is your politics, I said. I made two others points about the ruling parties and their student politics. I said they dabble in politics only to secure their careers. They have nothing to do with bringing about social change, speaking up for the poor or bringing order in a chaotic world. Their only purpose is to win elections, secure their political future and maybe even become a cabinet minister. The students' union is the stepping stone to the cabinet. If a student organization says one thing and does another, it can never win people's confidence, I concluded. In the question hour the ABVP candidate couldn't come up with adequate responses; he stuttered initially and then fell silent.

My speech in the presidential debate seemed to have touched a chord. Students rose above their organizational loyalties and cheered me. People greeted me with greater warmth. The mood had changed in the campus and I could sense the tide was turning towards me.

But I still did not imagine that I'd win the election. This was perhaps the first time that the AISF had fought an election by itself and won. The results would be announced on the third day after elections. For three days and nights I hadn't had a wink of sleep but when the results came I felt full of adrenalin, unable to think of rest. I also felt an immense burden of expectation on my shoulders. JNU students had given me a big responsibility in a very difficult time. I couldn't let them down.

26

Over the year, the BJP government had made a number of troubling appointments across universities and institutes in the country to culturally take control of these organizations. Many of these appointees had no real qualifications except for their association with the RSS and they weren't accepted or respected by the academic and student bodies. The first move was made at the Film and Television Institute of India (FTII) at Pune where the sole qualification of the person appointed chairman was that he followed Modi's ideology. The FTII student body began a protest.

The Indian Council of Historical Research (ICHR) was next, where many of its board members resigned in protest. Then there was a row at the prestigious Indian Institutes of Technology (IITs). A situation was created where the heads were expected to either toe the line or go home. In June 2015, sanctions were imposed on the

Ambedkar Periyar Study Circle (APSC) in IIT Madras. The activists at IIT Madras began to agitate, and soon the FTII protest joined them.

The unity that I had been talking about for the past year now became more relevant than ever. So when I won the elections, I did not take out a victory procession that night as was the tradition. Instead, when I took the oath, I said I would organize a unity procession that raised the flags of all student parties except the ABVP. The march was a success. More than 1500 students took part, coming from the left and Ambedkarite organizations. The campus was charged by the clamour of our voices, the energy in our vision. But most importantly we won everyone's hearts by making the election victory not just the AISF's but that of all left-leaning, egalitarian-minded parties.

The government had come to power promising the creation of two crore jobs to the young, and improving the education system. But it was instead conducting a two-pronged attack on students. There was the attempt to control the various universities and institutes around the country. They then fixed their gaze on educational scholarships. The Scholarship Enhancement Committee was set up to look into the matter. It recommended doing away with non-NET scholarship, that is, the University Grants Commission (UGC) scholarships for research scholars in the central universities.

JNU immediately reacted to this decision. Our view was that the fellowship was a question of Dalits, backward classes, women, minorities and the poor. Discontinuing the fellowship was not going to affect those whose parents earned Rs 5 lakh a month. But a student whose family earned Rs 5000 would have to give up her studies. In this country who is poor? It's clear – Dalits, backward classes, Muslims, adivasis. In a society where girls are married off before the age of fifteen, how would girls study if there wasn't a robust system of scholarships? Why was it stopped? Because the government wanted to privatize education. This is how neo-liberalism works. And through privatization, hard-earned reservations for the deprived sections are also being diminished.

A demonstration was held outside the UGC office in Delhi. For the first time I saw JNU students getting so agitated – breaking down the main gate, protesters parked themselves inside the UGC compound. This agitation gave birth to a new phrase – Occupy UGC, echoing the protest movement against Wall Street. When we began our agitations, none of us had imagined it would become so big. Occupy UGC gradually turned into a national movement and students from all over the country united over the issue.

Smriti Irani was the human resource development (HRD) minister under whom come the affairs of education. She met the protesters just once. More than 5000 students from all over the country had collected in Delhi to march in protest to her office. The police tried their best to stop them but when the public is determined no police force can stop them.

Mantriji had to come out on the road. At first we were surprised that she did. Later we realized that she'd done so because there was a lot of media gathered outside. Still I must praise her because no minister in this government has the courage to come on to the road and talk to the public.

The meeting, however, was of no use. What was more important for Irani were the lights and camera. Lighting up a poor man's life was not on her agenda. Had it been so she could have met us away from the media and tried to resolve the issue. She came to JNU once, but quietly, and sanctioned one exhaust fan for the canteen at the students' union building. This fan doesn't 'exhaust' any air; it appears it has been put there to exhaust our aspirations. Her relations with the students steadily declined and after Rohith Vemula's suicide in January 2016 there was a complete breakdown.

Occupy UGC became a platform for creative and original protest. Songs, skits and poems were presented at the venue. Teachers from JNU and other institutions held classes there. Through the winter season, students sat on dharna round the clock. The police had also become more aggressive with us, after the BJP came to power. A minor argument with the students and they would start a lathi charge. During the Occupy UGC days this happened several times and many got hurt. More than a dozen students were hospitalized.

What shocked us all was seeing male cops beating up women students. This was the height of oppression. In JNU students fight for their convictions, it is not a conspiracy against the police or the government. All they want to know is why their rights are being taken away. But the police and government treat them like their enemies. They look at them not as students of the country but enemies at the border. It is a strange paradox. The government talks eloquently of vasudhaiva kutumbakam – the world is one family. And at the same time they brutally beat up their own people.

During the UGC protest we saw, for the first time, the possibility of unity. It is not easy to mobilize students. The university years are ones when everyone lives in a world of their own, looking at things in their own individual way. The world outside doesn't matter as much. But now the threat was real and students were beginning to converge to the view that the BJP government was anti education, constitution and democracy.

This helped in bringing them together. People with different ideologies and from different affiliations sat together by the roadside. Sleeping on tarpaulin sheets, lighting bonfires to stay warm, chanting slogans, singing songs – these were the varied experiences of the movement.

It was Dussehra, and the effigy of Ravana was being burnt in many parts of the country. Modiji too was going to set fire to Ravana's effigy. He was to drive past the UGC office on his way to the Red Fort. It seemed very strange that the symbol of evil of our time was himself going to set fire to an alleged symbol of evil from different times.

There was heavy deployment of police. That day we saw how terrified people in power are. We were just a handful of students, not more than a hundred, but a large force was deployed around us. Perhaps they thought we were going to pelt stones at them.

The thought of burning an effigy ourselves came to our minds. We decided to build a sculpture of the central government with jute bags and old clothes. Bringing it to the venue proved to be more challenging. We had to hide it as though it was a missile. Playing hide-and-seek with the police, our supporters managed to smuggle it to the UGC office. We then set it on fire. That day we learnt the lesson that no matter how powerful your rulers may be, if the public is united it can do anything. The effigy was burning and we were seeing the flames of a revolution rising.

Late that night, the police attacked us. We were about a hundred. They were three times as many. We had occupied UGC. They had come to occupy us. The police forced us into buses and dropped us at Bhalswa thana. The officer there was a good man. He was happy to see students in his thana, a first, instead of the usual criminals. He welcomed us as though we were baraatis.

Up till now whenever we were taken into custody it was at Sansad Marg or Chanakyapuri. Sansad Marg since our protests took place outside Parliament or Jantar Mantar, and Chanakyapuri since it was outside the embassies. I have been taken into custody in Patna also for similar protests. But there is a difference between Delhi and Patna police. The Delhi police offers you tea, whereas the Patna police hurls filthy abuses at you.

It wasn't just the cops in the station. The cops manning the UGC, initially so hostile to us, had also begun to soften. It was winter. We used to sit all night long by the roadside, shivering in the cold. The police jawans used to give us wood to burn at night to keep us warm. But they didn't approach us directly to give the wood, they would just keep it quietly near where we were sitting.

It wasn't just the cops who surprised us. A favourite tactic to tire out protesters is to cut off their supplies. In the Occupy UGC days, the bathrooms in the premises were locked up. Electricity was also disconnected. Girls were the backbone of this movement; in fact, there were always more girl protesters than boys in our movements. The inconveniences began to get to them.

What a major issue this is for girls who wish to be in public life and politics. How difficult it is for them to participate in processions and protests if they cannot attend to the call of nature. The government which supposedly believes in *beti bachao, beti padhao* has not only discontinued their fellowship, it has also locked up the toilets for them. Ironically, this government spends lakhs and crores on advertisements for making toilets for women.

Right outside the UGC building there is a temple and a mosque. Women protesters first tried using the toilet in the temple thinking it might be difficult for them to enter the mosque. But they were not allowed inside. Not seeing any other alternative, we tried the mosque. They opened their doors for us round the clock.

Right through Occupy UGC, the mosque remained our lifeline. It became an active participant in the movement. The occupants of the mosque had to bear the brunt of this when at three o'clock at night the police raided the premises, carried out a search and harassed the attendants. Despite such difficulties, they continued supporting the students. To stop them, the police even threatened to have ongoing construction work there stopped. But the mosque stood firm.

27

During Occupy UGC I went to three states to rally the campuses there – Bihar, Jharkhand and West Bengal. In Bihar the sentiment was, as expected, against the central government and we got very positive responses there. But Jharkhand was a problem and in Ranchi University and other campuses the ABVP tried to disrupt our programme.

This was nothing new. During the UGC movement we saw the president of the DU students' union, who was from the ABVP, throw stones at us inside the UGC campus at night. In Ranchi University they came to disrupt our programme but because of the huge presence of students there they could do nothing. In Bihar and West Bengal, they couldn't muster up the courage. How can we call them a students' organization! Stone pelting, throwing shoes, using abusive language, beating up people – such acts of thuggery are their trademark.

I met innumerable students and teachers and it opened my eyes to the problems that Indian university students had to face. I saw that it was not just JNU that was struggling with the problem of lack of accommodation. At least JNU has some hostels. There are universities around the country that don't have any hostels at all. Right next to us there is DU, where the ABVP has been in power for years. There hostel accommodation is available only for a few thousand students, whereas the number of students there is in lakhs.

The same is true of student funding. In JNU at least all students get non-NET fellowships. There are many universities and colleges where students get no scholarships at all. We at least have a library. In many places there is no library. I returned from my trips convinced more than ever of the need to unite and fight.

In the long history of students' conflict with this government, the Occupy UGC movement was a landmark. Here students came face-to-face with the ministry. The movement was full of promise and slowly the entire nation began to get involved.

One reason it was successful is that although we kick-started the movement at JNU, we pulled in many universities together, ensuring that no one leader or organization would get all the power. JNU acted as the backbone but we didn't hog credit for its success. A democratic committee took decisions and implemented them.

For a political worker this was a very exciting phase. You didn't have to mobilize people – they came by themselves and pulled you in their wave. Studies were far away from my mind. My personal needs didn't seem significant. That winter, we had meetings all night long on footpaths and under the open skies, and all we would think of was our next move. We would argue, criticize each other, often disagree with each other – but in the end we'd reach a consensus. New friends were being made; old bonds were strengthened. All of us who didn't agree politically were learning to work together.

The government couldn't finish off the movement in Delhi. So it began to target students in other cities. The action against the students of Hyderabad Central University (HCU) was an outcome of this.

Reservation has created a diverse student body in Indian universities and these students had begun to raise their concerns in the classrooms. For instance, when adivasi students were studying history they wanted to know why their history was not being taught. Students from Dalit and backward classes argued that caste was not a structure created by the British – it had been part of our culture for thousands of years. In addition to Gandhi and Marx, young people had begun to read Ambedkar.

In HCU, the leftist SFI and Ambedkar Students' Association (ASA) came together against the ABVP. When a documentary made on the controversial Muzaffarnagar riots of 2013 was screened nationwide, the ABVP was up in arms, and attacked the screening of the film in Delhi. In Hyderabad, they made a fiery young Dalit activist called Rohith Vemula and his friends who were part of the ASA, their target. A long process of inquiries against them was initiated in which everyone from the HRD ministry to the university administration was involved. A ban was imposed on five of them including Vemula.

At JNU we were outraged and sat in dharna with the Hyderabad students in solidarity and decided to hold a protest demonstration on 18 January outside the HRD ministry. But on the 17th evening, news of Rohith Vemula's suicide broke out. His eloquent suicide note said: 'The value of a man is reduced to his immediate identity. To a vote. To a number. Never was a man treated as a mind. As a glorious thing made up of stardust.'

Our demonstration became a movement. People collected in huge numbers for 'Justice for Rohith Vemula' and it spread nationwide. We received lots of support – much of it invisible. A bread pakora seller fed us pakoras. Comrades who were hurt by the police and by Sanghi goondas were quietly given free treatment by a doctor.

If a movement touches people's imagination and talks of their problems in the right way and at the right time, it turns into something big. In the past the great people's movements were often initiated from the top, through strong leadership. Now the pattern is different – today, small movements from different places join together to make a popular people's movement.

There are two reasons for this. First, it shows the inability of electoral politics in addressing people's issues. Everywhere people have their own particular problems but these are often not resolved by the leaders. The discontent leads to small local movements which aren't given much importance. But slowly the people leading these movements realize that there are others like them who face similar problems. That they have one opponent. And so they come together and the movement becomes big. It is a must that people come together. I believe that farmers must raise the issues of writers and writers must raise the issues of farmers.

The second reason is that students are probably the only community today which stay together in large numbers. Many young people have managed to secure higher education through reservations and scholarships. The trend towards privatizing education and scrapping funding means that many find they are on shaky ground from the minute they arrive at university.

177

At the same time, this class of young people arrive in these institutes with a different world view – they are looking at their own backgrounds, their societies with an educated and questioning eye like Rohith Vemula did. That is why they are taking to the streets.

They remain connected to their communities so when they agitate their communities join in their movement and a student agitation turns into society's movement. That is why higher education institutes, especially the universities, throughout the country are becoming battlefields.

The government was petrified of this unprecedented unity among students and the oppressed. Everyone involved in this movement was on their hit list. Especially JNU, which was always their target anyway. It wasn't just the ABVP, from the RSS magazine *Panchjanya* to Subramaniam Swamy, everyone was after JNU.

It was said that terrorists lived in the university and that the Border Security Force should be posted here. All hostels had to be vacated and sanitized. Funding for JNU was reduced. But the Justice for Rohith Vermula movement continued, taking on proportions of a public movement. And then 9 February happened.

Part 5

Tihar

28

On 8 February, the students' union had organized a cultural programme featuring the people's singer Sheetal Sathe and her troupe. Sheetal Sathe and her husband, Sachin Mali, were also under arrest for alleged Maoist connections. Sheetal was out on bail but her husband was still in jail. The programme went on till late at night and it was almost two o'clock by the time everyone left.

It had been a long, busy day spent in preparation for the programme. The past few days had been hectic too. I had been in Rourkela for a few days for a youth conference. I returned on the 7th and had attended Sheetal Sathe's programme at the Press Club. There was a lot of sleep to catch up on. Putting my phone to charge, I hit the bed. A few friends had accompanied me to my room. Leaving me to rest, they switched off the lights and also, without realizing it, the electric board to which my phone charger was connected.

I ended up sleeping undisturbed all of the next day and woke up only in the evening. As always, I checked my phone on waking up but saw it was dead. So I transferred the SIM to my old phone, freshened up, and went to the tea shop. It was 5.30 p.m.

I was having a paratha and tea when someone passing by said, 'What kind of president are you? People are beating each other up at Sabarmati dhaba and you're sitting here drinking tea?'

I said, 'It's not the president's job to stop people from beating up one another. That is the job of the security guard.'

He told me this was no ordinary fight – the ABVP was harassing the organizers of a cultural programme at Sabarmati dhaba. Just then I saw an ABVP student from my hostel, Brahmaputra, running out of the hostel. From his speed I could tell that the matter was serious. I too made my way to Sabarmati.

Standing near the dhaba, ABVP people were shouting slogans: *Khoon se tilak karange, golion se aarti. Pukarti, pukarti, Ma Bharati pukarti.* (We will apply the tilak with blood and perform the aarti with bullets. Mother India is calling.) One of them came to me and said tauntingly, 'Where were you, president sahib? See what's going on.'

When I asked him what was going on, he replied, 'Afzal Guru's *barsi* [death anniversary] is being celebrated.'

I didn't believe him. Accused of involvement in the 2001 Parliament attack, Guru had been jailed and eventually hanged.

I asked why anyone would celebrate Afzal Guru's barsi. He quickly backtracked and said, 'A cultural programme is being organized here. We are here to oppose that.'

I said, okay, carry on opposing but I had heard that the fight had become physical. He said there was no violence, that they were just opposing the programme peacefully.

About fifty metres away students had formed a ring. They were not doing anything. Within the ring, a girl was standing on a bench with a book in her hand and talking to the gathering. I looked around. There was a police vehicle parked nearby and some cops in plain clothes.

After some time, the procession moved towards the road and headed for Ganga dhaba. The ABVP group tried to stop them. I asked the security guards to form a chain and separate the two groups to prevent them from fighting. A fight was avoided. There were some arguments but no clash.

There were about a hundred policemen waiting at Ganga dhaba, along with the Vasant Kunj thana's station house officer (SHO), or cop in charge. On one side was the ABVP group and on the other students not affiliated to any one party. Both sides were sloganeering. *ABVP murdabad, Gundagardi nahi chalegi, JNU hai chhatron ka, ABVP ki jagir nahi,* shouted one group. (Death to the ABVP. JNU is not their property. JNU belongs to the students. It's no place for thuggery.)

The ABVP was chanting: *Jahan hue balidaan Mukherjee woh Kashmir hamara hai, Jo Kashmir hamara hai, woh sara ka sara hai, Cheen ke dalalon ko, dhakke maaro saalon ko.* (Where [Syama Prasad] Mukherjee laid down his life that Kashmir is ours, the Kashmir that's ours is completely ours. Push away these pimps of China.)

The senior police officer asked me to address the crowd and get them to leave. I realized I needed to defuse the anger of the students against the ABVP and find a way to ease the tension. I didn't know what had happened at the programme or what slogans had been raised. But my experience told me that the ABVP tries to disrupt any programme which goes against their ideology. I also felt that it was the democratic right of the organizers to organize the programme, even if I did not agree with them.

I said, the ABVP were fledgling RSS wannabes and there was no need to take them seriously. What could these poor people do? They were waiting for Modi's acche din, the good days that he had promised in his election slogans, to come. But the good days never did come. So they had to now get at least an ad hoc job like this one.

There was so much unemployment and one needed to sympathize with their hardship.

My mockery lightened the mood of the students assembled there, which was my intention. Then I made sarcastic comments on the wider politics prevalent in the country and our new vice chancellor who was an appointee of the BJP. Gradually the crowd dispersed.

The security guards filled me in. They said that the students had planned a cultural programme – as I had suspected – to question the unconstitutional manner in which Guru had been killed. But the administration had refused permission. The organizers had decided to continue nonetheless. Mikes couldn't be put up; posters were not allowed. So they read out poetry without mikes. Then they got ready for a march. The ABVP tried to stop all this.

In the recent past the ABVP has done this several times. When *Caste on the Menu Card* and *Muzaffarnagar Baaki Hai* were being screened the ABVP had created a similar hungama. They had also tried to stop the documentary made on FTII. Earlier the ABVP would act on its own. Now with their government at the centre, they roped in the administration to disrupt activities. I remember a few years ago some students had prepared a programme on the history of asuras. The ABVP tried to stop this because Mahisasur, the enemy of Goddess Durga, was being celebrated. This is typical of them.

The same night I attended the meeting (AO) of all organizations that I had called earlier. It was about the students' union elections, which in my presidential speech I had promised would be held under the JNUSU's constitution. As noted earlier, elections in JNU are held according to the recommendations of the Lyngdoh Committee. At the end of the meeting, a student told me that the ABVP had gone to the thana to complain about the evening's programme.

Representatives of all parties said that the students' union should go and find out what was going on. What did the police have to do with this? About ten of us went to the thana. The ABVP group was already there. When I asked why they were there, they said they'd come to file a complaint of manhandling.

I said there hadn't been any such fights. If they had a problem with the programme, they should report it to the university administration. Nothing had taken place that required police intervention.

Had they had a medical legal certificate (MLC) made, which was necessary to lodge such a complaint? They hadn't. I asked the police for a copy of the complaint. It came as a shock to me. Those listed as culprits were the leading activists in the campus, handpicked from each major organization of the campus except the ABVP.

Most were Dalits, women or Muslims or belonged to the backward classes.

We returned from the thana. At the time I thought this was a case of simple harassment, the usual that I had come to expect from the ABVP. I had no idea that a well-hatched conspiracy was at work.

29

A phone call woke me up the next morning. It was from a TV channel. They were asking for my comments on Afzal Guru's barsi being celebrated in JNU and the anti-national slogans that were chanted. Anti-national slogans? In JNU? I was shocked to hear this. The person on the line was sure they had been raised and wanted to interview me over the phone. I agreed. The call was transferred.

Once again the question was repeated. I too repeated what I had said before – that Afzal Guru's barsi had not been celebrated in JNU and that if anyone had chanted anti-national slogans I would condemn it strongly. The ABVP was making this all up just as it had on earlier occasions. Instead of fighting for the rights of students, it was working like the government's spy.

The phone didn't stop ringing thereafter. Initially all the TV channels interviewed me on the phone until

News 24 invited me to their studio for the *5 Ki Panchayat* show. Soon the other channels wanted me to appear in their studios in the same slot. I started to worry now and wondered what was going on. Actually I don't watch TV. There is a common TV in the hostel but I never have the time for it. Neither did I have Internet in my room, and I hadn't seen the day's papers either.

When a car arrived from News 24 to take me to the studio I was informed that an ABVP representative would also be appearing for the same show and asked if I had any problem sharing the car with him. I had no problem with that.

The car reached the administrative block to pick him up. There the ABVP was demonstrating against the university administration, demanding action against the organizers of the programme. The representative got into the car. We chatted on the way to the studio. He was carrying chana, which he shared with me. I had no idea that even as he was offering me chana, his government was planning to feed me chana in the prison.

In the studio there was one person from the Hindu Mahasabha and a Congress leader. That was the first time I saw the video of 9 February that was being circulated everywhere and which had led to the media frenzy. Slogans attacking India and supporting Kashmir's battle for azadi were being chanted. I couldn't believe that this had happened in JNU. I said that, first, I wasn't convinced that such sloganeering could happen in JNU. Second, even if it had, I did not support it. But I also questioned why the ABVP was trying to twist this whole situation in its favour. It was an attempt to poison the entire campus.

It became clear to me that this was an attack on JNU. The ABVP has always wanted to exclude the poor from education. Because when sons and daughters of those who earn Rs 3000 a month do a PhD they will begin to ask difficult questions. At the same time the Justice for Rohith Vemula movement was still ongoing and this was clearly being used as a diversion.

The discussion ended and before I left the studio a man from Zee News came running and requested me to go to their studio for just ten minutes. The discussion on Zee News had already begun when I got there. But the way the anchor was speaking, it was as if he was himself the witness, the jury and the judge. My first question was to him – who pays you, Zee News or the RSS?

By this time, I was beginning to doubt the authenticity of the video. On the night of 9 February I had seen a Zee News cameraman at Ganga dhaba. They must have shot some raw videos. But raw is raw – it is real. What is shown on TV is edited and possibly tinkered with.

I had started being trolled on Facebook and WhatsApp. I was receiving abusive messages from unknown numbers.

These people had strange names, like Bhakt, Old Monk, etc. That night it became impossible to get any calls on my phone. I suspected that either the company had blocked my number or the network was crowded.

The next day, 11 February, the JNU students' union took two actions. We distributed pamphlets which condemned the slogans if the videos were indeed true. We also led a demonstration against the ABVP, accusing it of playing dirty in the campus and outside it, deliberately wanting to malign the image of JNU because it was a progressive university.

There was unprecedented media presence for our demonstration. There seemed to be more journalists there than students. We met the VC and demanded a full and fair inquiry into the matter. The VC informed us that a high-level committee had been set up.

We asked him for the names of the members of the committee. The VC said he was not aware of the names and that the registrar would know. We found this odd – after all, the VC had set up the committee. We also thought it was unusual that the VC had not asked for the traditional proctorial inquiry. His reply was that since the media had blown it out of proportion it was necessary to resolve the issue quickly.

We demanded that the committee be comprised of representatives of all schools and socially backward sections. I was suspicious that history would repeat itself here as in the Rohith Vemula case where the inquiry committee didn't see fair representation. My suspicion was not without ground. Just a few days ago we had sat on hunger strike in JNU in support of Justice for Rohith Vemula. While this was on someone had written Jai Bhim on the wall of the admin building in front of which we were striking. This is common practice here. But the proctor's office issued a notice to the student. Our worries proved to be true. When we went to meet the registrar, he told us the names of the three committee members. All three had been accused of weakening social justice in the campus. We demanded that there should be a five-member committee having representation from deprived sections and that it should look into every aspect of why the programme had been cancelled and who had cancelled it. Who had called the media? The videos too had to be validated. We also wanted to look at the origin of the crisis – it was troubling that permission was given to the students to hold their meet and then refused on the insistence of the ABVP.

After leaving the registrar's office, I addressed the students who were still demonstrating downstairs. I shared the union's stance with them. I spoke on two issues. The first was that the RSS in their talk of anti-nationalism was deciding what was patriotic and what was not. What moral right did it have when it had not even participated in the country's freedom struggle? I wanted to target this history of theirs.

I also wanted to emphasize that the sloganeering was wrong and it was the failure of the JNU administration and the police that such slogans were raised in their presence, if they had been raised at all. Instead of addressing the concerns of students regarding their failures in acting democratically and responsibly, they were trying to get political mileage from the event. I wanted to unmask this hypocrisy.

This is what I said:

They are the ones who burnt the Tricolour. They are followers of Savarkar who apologized to the British. They are the ones who, in Haryana, have changed the name of one airport. There was one airport named after Bhagat Singh. The Khattar government has now named it after one Sanghi (a person associated with the RSS).

What I mean to say is that we don't need the certificate of patriotism from the RSS. We don't need a nationalist certificate from the RSS. We belong to this country. We love this country. We fight for the 80 per cent of the poor population of this country. For us, this is nation worship.

We have full faith in Babasahab (Ambedkar). We

have full faith in the Constitution of India. We want to say this very forcefully that if anyone tries to challenge the Constitution, be it the Sanghis, we will not tolerate.

We have faith in the Constitution. But we don't have faith in the Constitution that is taught in Jhandewalan (RSS headquarters in Delhi) and Nagpur. We don't have faith in Manusmriti, we don't have faith in the caste system in this country.

The Constitution and Babasahab Ambedkar talk about corrective measures. The same Babasahab Ambedkar talks about abolishing capital punishment. The same Babasahab Ambedkar talks about freedom of expression. And we want to uphold the Constitution, we want to uphold our right.

But it's shameful and sad that the ABVP, in association with their media friends, is running an orchestrated campaign.

Yesterday, the ABVP joint secretary said that [they] fight for fellowships. How ridiculous it sounds! Their government, Madam ManuSmriti Irani is ending fellowship and they [claim to be] fighting for fellowships. Their government has reduced the higher education budget by 17 per cent.

Our hostel has not been built for the past four years, there is no Wi-fi. BHEL gave us one bus but the administration has no money for oil. And ABVP people stand like Dev Anand claiming that they will get hostels built, they will get Wi-fi and they will get fellowships.

They will be exposed if there is a debate on the basic issues in this country. We are proud of being JNU-ites because we discuss and debate the basic issues concerning this country. We raise issues related to the dignity of women, Dalits, tribals and minorities in this country. And so, their Swamy (Subramanian Swamy) says that jihadis live in JNU, that JNU students spread violence.

On behalf of JNU, I want to challenge RSS ideologues. Call [them] and hold a debate. We want to debate the concept of violence. We want to raise questions about the frenzied ABVP's slogans, their slogan that they will do tilak with blood and aarti with bullets. Whose blood do they want to spill? They aligned with the British and fired bullets on the freedom fighters of this country. They fired bullets when poor people demanded bread; they fired bullets when people dying of hunger talked about their rights; they have fired bullets on Muslims; they have fired bullets on women when they demand equal rights.

They say that five fingers are not equal. They advocate that women should emulate Sita and give agnipariksha. There is democracy in this country, and democracy gives equal rights to all – be it a student, a worker, the poor or the rich, Ambani or Adani. And when we talk about equal rights of women, they accuse us of destroying Indian culture.

We want to destroy the culture of exploitation, the culture of caste, the culture of Manuwad and Brahminism. [Your definition of culture shall not determine the definition of our culture.] They have a problem when people of this country talk about democracy, when they give blue salute along with red salute, when people talk about [Babasaheb] Ambedkar along with Marx, when people talk about Asfaqulla Khan (the freedom fighter). They can't tolerate. It is their conspiracy. They were British stooges. I dare them to file a defamation case against me. I say that the RSS's history is of siding with the British. These traitors today are distributing certificates of nationalism.

Check my mobile phone, friends. Dirty abuses are being hurled at my mother and sister. Which Mother India are you talking about? If my mother is not part of your Mother India, your concept of Mother India is not acceptable to me.

My mother is an Anganwadi sewika, my family runs with the Rs 3,000 she earns and they are abusing her. I'm ashamed that in this country, the mothers of the poor, Dalit farmers are not part of Mother India. I will hail the mothers of this country, I will hail the fathers of this country, I will hail the mothers and sisters of this country, I will hail the poor farmers, Dalits, tribals and labourers. I will tell them that if they have courage, then say 'Inquilab zindabad', say 'Bhagat Singh zindabad', say 'Sukhdev zindabad', say 'Asfaqulla Khan zindabad', say 'Babasahab Ambedkar zindabad'. Only then will I believe that you have faith in this country.

They are enacting the drama of celebrating Ambedkar's 125th birth anniversary. If they have courage, they should raise the issues Ambedkar raised. Caste system is one of the biggest problems in this country. Talk about caste system, bring reservation in every sector, bring reservation in the private sector. Raise these questions, then I will believe that you have faith in this country.

This nation had never been yours and will never be yours. A nation is made by its people and if there is no place for hungry and poor people in your idea of the nation, then it is no nation.

Yesterday, I said in one TV debate that we are in difficult times. The way fascism is coming in the country, even the media would not be spared. The media would be provided with written scripts from the RSS office, just as written scripts came from the Congress office during the Emergency.

Some media friends told me that JNU runs on

taxpayers' money, on subsidy. Yes, it is right that JNU runs on subsidy. But I want to raise the question: what are universities for? Universities are there for critical analysis of the society's collective conscience. Critical analysis should be promoted. If universities fail in their duty, there would be no nation. If people are not part of a nation, it will turn into a grazing ground for the rich, for exploitation and looting.

If we don't assimilate people's culture, beliefs and rights, a nation would not be formed. We stand firmly with the country, we stand for the dreams of Bhagat Singh and Babasahab Ambedkar. We stand for equal rights. We stand for the right to live. Rohith (Vemula) had to lose his life to stand for these rights.

But we want to tell these Sanghis – 'shame on your government'. We challenge the central government – we will not allow in JNU whatever it did in the case of Rohith. Rohith will not lose his life here. We will not forget Rohith's sacrifice. We will stand for freedom of expression.

Leave aside Pakistan and Bangladesh, we call for unity of the poor and the toiling masses of the world. We hail the humanity of this world, we hail the humanity of India.

We have identified those who are against humanity. This is the biggest issue before us today. We have identified that face of casteism, the face of Manuwad, the face of the nexus between Brahminism and capitalism. And we have to expose these faces. We have to usher in real freedom, and that freedom will come through the Constitution, through Parliament. And we will achieve it.

I want to appeal to you friends that despite all the differences, we have to safeguard this freedom of expression, we have to safeguard our Constitution, we have to safeguard the unity and integrity of this country. For this, we have to remain united and fight the forces trying to divide our country, the forces that give shelter to terrorists.

One last question before I end my speech. Who is Kasab? Who is Afzal Guru? Who are these people, who are in a state to wrap bombs around their body and kill? If these questions are not raised in universities, the existence of universities becomes pointless. If we don't define justice, if we don't define violence and how we see violence? Violence is not only about killing somebody with a gun. There is violence when the JNU administration denies the constitutional rights guaranteed to Dalits. This is institutional violence.

They talk about justice. Who will decide what justice is? Brahminism did not allow Dalits to enter temples. The British did not allow dogs and Indians to enter restaurants. That was justice then. We challenged that justice and today we challenge the justice of the ABVP and the RSS because their justice does not accommodate justice for us. If their justice doesn't accommodate justice for us, we will not accept their justice and this freedom. We will accept this freedom when every person gets his constitutional right. We will accept justice when there is equal rights for all.

Friends, the situation is very serious. Under no circumstances does the JNUSU (the JNU students' union) support any violence, any terrorist, any terror incident and any anti-India activity. I want to reiterate that the JNUSU strongly condemns slogans of 'Pakistan zindabad' raised by some unidentified people.

I want to share one thing with you, friends. It is a question related to the JNU administration and the ABVP. Thousands of things take place on this JNU campus. Listen carefully to the slogans being raised by the ABVP now. They are calling us 'communist dogs'. They are calling us 'Afzal Guru's dogs'. They are calling us 'children of jihadis'. If the Constitution gives us the right to be citizens, then is it not an attack on our constitutional right when they call our parents dogs? We want to ask this question to the ABVP and the JNU administration.

We want to ask the JNU administration for whom, with whom and on what basis it works. It is now clear that the JNU administration first gives permission and then withdraws it on receiving a call from Nagpur. This thing of first giving permission and then withdrawing, it has intensified. First, they will announce fellowship and then tell that it has been withdrawn. This is the RSS and ABVP pattern with which they want to run this country.

We want to ask the JNU administration. Permission (for the February 9 programme where eventually the [alleged] anti-India slogans were shouted) was granted despite the fact that posters had been put up and pamphlets distributed. When it gave permission, on whose directive was it withdrawn? We want to ask this to the JNU administration.

At the same time, understand the truth of these (ABVP) people. Don't hate them. I feel sad for them. They are jumping today because they feel that the way they got Gajendra Chauhan (in the FTII), they would get people like him in every institution. They feel that with people like Chauhan everywhere, they would get jobs. Once they get jobs, they will forget nation worship and Bharat Mata. What to tell of the Tricolour, which they have never respected? They will also forget the saffron flag.

I want to know what kind of nation worship they are talking about? If an owner doesn't behave properly with his employees, if a farmer doesn't do justice with his workers, if a highly paid CEO of a media house doesn't behave properly with the meagrely paid reporters, then what is this nation worship?

Their nation worship ends with an India-Pakistan cricket match. After that when they go out on the road, they misbehave with the person selling bananas. When the person selling bananas tells them that a dozen comes for Rs 40, they abuse him and accuse him of looting customers. They demand a dozen for Rs 30.

The day the person selling bananas turns and tells them that you are the real looters, they will term the poor fellow anti-national. Nation worship begins and ends with wealth and facilities. I know a number of ABVP people and I ask them whether the fervour of nationalism moves them? They tell me: 'What to do, brother, this government is for five years and two years are already over. Three years' talktime is left and whatever has to be done, should be done in this period.'

But I ask them what will happen if, tomorrow, one of their own members, who is going around in trains checking for beef, holds them by the collar and accuses them of being anti-national since they are from JNU? They could be lynched. I ask them whether they realize this danger?

They tell me that they realize this danger and so are opposing #JNUShutdown (a Twitter hashtag). First, they build an atmosphere against JNU and, then, oppose it when they realize that ultimately they have to live in JNU only.

This is why I want to tell all JNU-ites that elections are coming in March. The ABVP people will seek your votes with the 'Om' flag. Ask them: 'We are jihadis, we are terrorists, we are anti-nationals and by taking our votes, [would not you] also become anti-national?' Do ask them these questions. I know when you ask them these questions, they will tell you, 'not you but a few people are anti-nationals'. Then ask them, 'why did they not tell this in the media then'? Ask them why their vice-chancellor and registrar too did not tell then?

Tell them that those few people too are saying that they did not raise slogans of 'Pakistan zindabad', nor did they support terrorism. Those few people are asking why at first permission was granted and then withdrawn and this is an attack on their democratic right? These few people are saying that if somewhere a democratic struggle is being fought, they will stand for it.

They will never understand this. But the people, who have gathered here on short notice, understand the issue. They will go around the campus and tell the students that the ABVP is not only breaking this country but also JNU and we will not allow this to happen.

Long live JNU. JNU will continue to actively

participate in all democratic struggles taking place across the country, continue to strengthen the voice of democracy, the voice of freedom and freedom of expression. We will struggle and win and defeat the traitors of this country. With these words, I thank you all and appeal for unity.

Jai Bhim, Lal Salaam.

(Translated by J.P. Yadav for The Telegraph*)*

After the demonstration wound up I gave a few more sound bites to TV channels. That night, on behalf of the union, I called a meeting of all organizations. The agenda was to maintain peace in the campus and wait patiently till the committee's report came out. After that we would take the next steps.

The meeting was still on when we were told that the police had entered the campus. I was surprised. Coming out of the union office, I took a round of the campus. While walking in the campus I saw some ABVP people. They told me that a BJP MP, Mahesh Girri, had lodged an FIR which had led to the impending police visit. No one had been named in this FIR. The campus was rife with rumours and the students were in a state of panic. I felt it was necessary to reach out to the students to assuage their fears. I spent a few hours mingling with them in the dhabas around campus and finally went to sleep at 4.15 a.m.

30

On the morning of 12 February, I woke up at about eleven thirty. As usual I went to the dhaba downstairs and then headed towards my school. On my way I saw some police cars parked near the Convention Centre. The SHO of the Vasant Kunj thana was standing there. I went up to him, shook hands and asked what the matter was. He said they were here in connection with the 9 February incident.

I reminded him that nothing so serious had happened that it required this kind of attention. I myself had gone to meet him that night but he had been asleep. The SHO told me that there was pressure from the top and the police needed to be involved. He asked me to accompany him as he wanted to ask me some questions, essential for the investigation. I agreed.

I got into the vehicle. On the way the police took my mobile phone from me. I told them I had one more phone and gave them that also. After a while they also took my wallet. I'd thought they'd take me to the local Vasant Kunj thana. But we were moving towards Hauz Khas. The cops were constantly getting calls on their phones. They were saying something to each other which I couldn't follow. There was a minor discussion about taking the wrong route, because this one had a traffic jam.

Eventually we stopped outside the Lodhi Road thana. One of them suggested covering my face. I was supposedly being taken for questioning. I wondered why my face had to be covered but I still didn't realize what was happening.

I was taken inside the thana and made to sit in a tiny room. Then the questioning started. The man who had brought me here spoke to me politely. But then another cop came in and said very rudely, 'This is your country and you shout slogans against it?'

I found this very strange. When did I shout slogans against the country? I have been shouting slogans against Modi and that's no secret. Had Modi now become the country? By now I was beginning to get the feeling that something was seriously wrong. On what grounds had I been arrested, I asked them. Where was the warrant?

'You'll get the warrant in jail,' he said. 'There, you'll get everything.'

After that he spoke to someone on the phone. He asked if he should arrest me.

After disconnecting his call, he asked for my father's number. I am bad at phone numbers – I don't even remember my own. Luckily I remembered Pitaji's since he had been the first to get a phone at home. Calling my father, the cop told him that I'd been arrested for 'sedition'.

It was the first time someone had spoken clearly about the charge against me. Hearing the words so starkly, I felt worried and emotional for the first time. Thoughts of my family came flooding to my mind. Seeing the look on my face, the officer asked a constable if I had eaten. I hadn't. He gave instructions to feed me. I refused to eat. I said I would go on a hunger strike.

That made no difference to him. He got my belt removed. I was photographed from all angles.

Then I was taken to Safdarjung hospital to have my medical tests done. Before getting me out of the vehicle they covered my face. No medical test was done in the hospital. The police did some paperwork; the doctor wasn't allowed to come near me. I was taken back to the car. The cloth over my face was removed. I was then taken to court.

It was my first time in a courtroom and it looked very different from the movies. Everyone stood up when the judge entered. The police told the magistrate that I was Kanhaiya. I had been shouting slogans against the country and had celebrated Afzal Guru's barsi. This is the charge against him, they said. We need police custody (PC) for five days.

The judge turned to me. I introduced myself and said that the police were lying. I had never shouted slogans against the country. Nor had I organized a programme commemorating Afzal Guru.

The inquiry officer (IO) said they had a video to prove their charge.

I asked the judge to check the facts before believing the police. I had no lawyer. I had been arrested without being informed. Nor had I been shown any warrant. I also said that I had voluntarily accompanied the police to the station.

I'm a student, I said, who has come to JNU to study despite many hardships. I fought for issues; I spoke against the government, but never against the country. This country and its Constitution were mine too.

The judge asked for the video to be shown. I was not present anywhere in it. Slogans were being shouted but these were not the ones that were being shown on TV.

The judge said, 'This boy is not raising slogans. Nor is he in the video.' The IO said that the boys who were sloganeering were my friends. I denied this but while I was still speaking, the IO said, 'Sir, he has even been to Kashmir.'

The judge said, 'So what? I have also been to Kashmir.'

I laughed a little to myself when I heard this exchange. It's true, what they say. One can find humour in the most unlikely of places.

The IO replied that he had witnesses to testify against me and that they were in the process of recording their statement. This was news to me. There were some lawyers sitting in the courtroom. After seeing the video, one of them came to me and said, 'Don't worry. If you don't have any lawyer I'm with you. You tell the judge that I'm your lawyer.'

I said so to the judge. The lawyer suggested I say to the judge that all the ongoing proceedings must be documented in his order. I did so. The judge said that you have expressed faith in the court, so have faith.

The judge wrote that the accused had been produced in court by the police but the video shown by them did not feature the accused. However, since the police had said that they had a witness, the court was granting PC for inquiry. The police requested for a five-day PC; they were granted three.

When they were taking me out of the courtroom I met a friend who had studied law. After that I met two more friends. They asked the police where I was being taken. That's when the media arrived. They surrounded me, asking, 'Kanhaiya Kumar, you have been arrested for sedition. What do you have to say about that?'

For the first time I realized that news of my arrest must be on TV. I was amused but also by now really worried about my family. They would be shocked to see me on TV, being paraded in this way. How would Pitaji take this news? He had a heart problem. My mother would as always take care of everyone, but how was she herself going to deal with it? But I was sure of one thing: they would never believe that I had done anything anti-national.

I have been taken into custody several times during protests but there had never been a case registered against me. I could see now that the speech I had made to the students on 11 February and my overall activism had led to this arrest. I had also opposed the Manmohan Singh government and its policies but had never been threatened in this way. My arrest was part of a much larger conspiracy. As soon as I realized this, I was at peace. I decided not to worry. Whatever happens, I'll deal with it, I said to myself. Let's see for how long untruth can survive in the face of truth.

I was put in a lockup. A CCTV camera was installed. An armed guard was stationed outside. There was nothing to sleep on. There was a blanket of some kind which acted as both the bedding and a cover. My chappals, jacket, etc. had been confiscated outside. I asked for my jacket as I was cold. They said they couldn't give it to me as it had a drawstring with which I might attempt suicide.

My cell had a bottle of water, a tap and a toilet seat. I had to make do with this for drinking, bathing, washing, etc. I tried talking to the police outside my cell. On my first night I was rebuffed. When I asked the guard on duty for some soap I was told this was not my hostel. Later his attitude changed completely. He started to get me drinking water and taking me to the bathroom for bathing.

On that first night I was visited by two men. They asked me to write down everything that had happened. I wrote down the entire sequence of events of 9 February. We talked for a while. As they left, one of them said that had he not been on duty he would have liked to talk to me for longer. I enjoyed talking to you, he said.

The police on the whole dealt with me well. They were beginning to understand that I was innocent and was being framed. Even those who were rude to begin with became much gentler in their dealings later on.

I could see one difference. Other than the IO all the other cops of the Vasant Kunj thana treated me very well, because they knew the truth. (I was lodged at the Lodhi Road thana for security reasons; the case against me was registered at the Vasant Kunj thana.) At the other thanas, opinions were formed about me on the basis of the TV coverage. And so their behaviour was different. Any of them who had a conversation with me even briefly revised their opinion.

I noticed something curious while in custody. The staff put on duty with me were either Dalit or Muslim. I am not sure, but I have a suspicion this was deliberate. A senior police officer I met at a Nagpur function shortly after being released confirmed that a secular force had been arranged for my security in that city. I didn't ask him what a secular force meant but when I read the names of the police personnel around me I knew he wasn't exaggerating. I saw this pattern repeated whenever I travelled after being freed.

Over time even the IO's attitude towards me began to soften and I wasn't taken in for any more questioning. Perhaps he had come to know more about me while making inquiries and had changed his mind. I will never know. The media on the outside, however, kept up their noise and their lies.

I had no real connect with the outside world over those three days and so it was hard to gauge what was happening. But seeing people's reaction to me was enough to tell me that the issue was still alive. I was taken for a medical check-up every day. Now that my face was not covered with a cloth, I could see the way people stared at me.

The doctor examining me would point me out to his staff during the medical check-ups. Look, this is Kanhaiya, he would say. He was surprised to see me docile and quiet with him. It appeared my image on TV was very different from what I was in real life.

The three-day remand was coming to an end. So far I had not been allowed to meet any of my friends and colleagues. I was told that I would not be produced in court. A special court was set up for me in the office of the deputy commissioner of police (DCP), South Delhi. The judge came there.

In the 'court hearing', the police asked for two more days to take my voice samples. The judge looked at my lawyer. Even before he could speak, I said I was ready to give them the voice samples. The police had no proof against me nor would they ever find any. The samples would be incontestable. Everyone could see once and for all that I had not done any sloganeering. Later in my cell I realized I had been naive. It wasn't wise to have so much faith in the police when they were acting on someone else's bidding. Nonetheless I gave the voice sample.

By now the police on duty had become very friendly with me. They even brought fruits for me and we'd sit together and eat them. During this time, I saw the hierarchical structure of the police from within. In the presence of the inspector everyone did 'sir-sir', but once he left, it was the sub-inspector who was called sir. Yet it was the constables who had to bear all expenses. The fruits, tea and snacks, all were arranged by them.

Sometimes they asked me if I'd go out and say that I was beaten up in custody. I couldn't understand their concern. Why would they care if I did such a thing? After all countless people left the police station with such stories. Only much later did I come to understand that they were seeing me on TV each day, that I was the burning issue, fought over and debated hotly on prime-time TV. What I said about them would count.

Occasionally a guard would ask, 'Kanhaiya, when you're released you won't forget us, will you?' They said, Kanhaiya, you wait and watch, one day you'll be a big man. It's a strange feeling to realize you've become famous (or maybe infamous) while sitting inside prison, locked away from the world.

31

Five days after being taken into custody, on the 17th, I learnt I was to be produced in court once again. On the day of my court appearance, a senior police officer told me I was going to get bail. I did not know then that the police commissioner had issued a statement saying that he would not oppose my bail petition. I said I wouldn't accept it. I had done nothing wrong that I should require bail. All charges against every student must be dropped. Nor did I know who would bail me out. The senior officer laughed and said, 'The entire university will be here for your bail.'

He asked me to write a statement that I had full faith in the Constitution and the judiciary, that I believed in the unity of India and that I would always strive towards keeping India united. I had no problem with writing this – they happened to be what I believed. I wrote it down in my own words. But the officer was not satisfied. He asked me to write the statement again. This time he told me what to write.

But on 17 February I was not given bail. The petition was not submitted at all.

Something else happened instead.

I was surprised at the level of preparation on the day. I couldn't understand it. Lots of cops, lots of vehicles. I realized the police were hiding me from the media. To go from the Lodhi Road thana to the Vasant Vihar thana, back lanes were used. On the way a constable said to me, chalo, we'll show you JNU today. The other said, he's going to be released, he'll go back to JNU in any case. But they took me to the Vasant Vihar thana via Baba Gang Nath Marg, driving past the main North Gate.

I was seeing my JNU after five days. The same nondescript entrance gate. Today it was heavily barricaded. A small demonstration was going on in which people I didn't know were participating. No one from JNU. On the other side of the road, a student I knew was walking. Passing my old haunts, seeing a familiar face pass me by, feeling near them and yet so far forcefully brought home to me the strange drama of my situation.

When we reached the Vasant Vihar thana, we went in by the back door, as had become customary. Then we were on our way to the court. Our convoy was stopped as we approached India Gate. We waited for almost half an hour. Phones were continuously ringing. Then the police took me to Patiala House Court.

There was an ocean of reporters and cameras. We were engulfed by the media. The cops asked me to sit with my head bent so no one could see me. Much later I discovered that the police had used dummies. They deployed four or five vehicles in which someone else sat with his head covered. The media ran after the dummies while I was quietly taken in another vehicle.

This is how the police played hide-and-seek with the media. The press eventually caught up with me and swarmed around my car. It was a mob. I had never been in the middle of a storm of people like this. Avoiding them, I was somehow taken inside the court premises.

As I walked in, a group of men dressed as lawyers – it was unclear if they were actually so – attacked me, abusing me loudly as they hit me. I fell down in the rush and confusion. My nose began to bleed. Some cops were also hurt. Somehow I managed to reach the courtroom safely with the help of the police. Some of the 'lawyers' were bold enough to enter the main room and were chased out.

I'll never forget that day. I was completely unprepared for the press mob outside. I had never experienced anything like this. The attack shook me even more. For the first time I became aware that my life could be in danger. Cut off from news for these five days, it now hit me with violent force how much of an issue my arrest had become. How hated a figure I was to some sections of society.

One of the men dressed as a lawyer was bold enough to enter the courtroom. He tried to hit me from behind. Another of my assailants entered and sat down on the court benches.

Many JNU teachers were present at the court. Worried at the sight of my dishevelled state and the anxiety on my face, one of them asked me what had happened. It was a relief to see familiar faces after the last few days. He calmed me down, making me drink some water. As soon as I relaxed a little, I told him that the man sitting behind me had beaten me up just outside the courtroom.

The police went up to the assailant and asked him, 'Who are you, bhai?' Instead of answering the question, he said boldly, 'Who are you?' The cop gave his name and asked for his identity proof. In return the man asked for the cop's ID. Then he got up and ran away. No one really pursued him despite my pleas. A woman lawyer I didn't know was present in the courtroom and she too was agitated that a lawbreaker could escape so easily from inside a courtroom.

I was taken to another room. The police were everywhere; no one was allowed to come in. Some lawyers were present in the room. I answered their questions and told them how I had been manhandled. Later I discovered that they were assigned by the Supreme Court. A doctor was called into the courtroom to treat my injuries. I told him how I had been beaten but the doctor didn't note down anything. He just stood there quietly, hearing me.

Seeing his attitude, the judge became angry and said that his licence could be cancelled if he didn't cooperate. The doctor started to make excuses but, now afraid, began to write.

The police had no reason to extend their remand, but since there was no application for bail, I was taken into judicial custody. This meant I would move from the lockup to jail. I was filled with real fear for the first time. What was happening outside? I had done nothing and if the police hadn't managed to find any evidence to implicate me, why was the media after me? Who were these people who had physically assaulted me and were trying to prove I was anti-national? I couldn't make any sense of any of it. It didn't help that there was such a large number of cops swarming all around me – it felt as if they were preparing for a war.

First one officer made me wear a helmet and guard. After a while he returned and took me to another room. Waiting for me there was another young cop who was about my build. We had to exchange our clothes. Now I was disguised in full police uniform.

From the courtroom, the court jail was not more than fifty metres away. All these elaborate arrangements were being made to cover this distance. The police were suspicious of its own people, worried that someone from the force itself might attack me. People stood around, talking heatedly to each other. Four hours went by in this fashion. I thought to myself, this is happening in the capital city, not in some remote area of the country. It felt like a bad dream. Then I was taken to the court jail.

The court jail was emptied for me. Now a strategy was being planned – how to take me to Tihar Jail. All the senior officers were arguing with each other. There were officers from different battalions. It was decided that any attacker would be shot at sight. A vehicle would be posted at every traffic signal and a green corridor would be created. First a dummy would be sent and when the media ran after it, my vehicle would speed past to Tihar.

TV crew from all the channels had gathered outside. Inside the court jail, I saw the news after many days. On the TV screen, the Delhi police commissioner was saying that they would not oppose my bail. He was showing the press the letter I had been made to write, in which I had vouched for my faith in the Constitution. Later I came to know that the police had given that letter out to the media under the title 'Kanhaiya ki Chithhi'. The letter and the question of bail would become matters for heated press debate.

Once again I was made to wear a helmet and guard, and to sit in the prisoner's van. There are separate sections in this van and police with different weapons – guns, tear gas, pepper spray – sit in the different sections. I was made to sit right behind the driver. The three cops sitting with me had no weapons. One of them said to me, don't worry, only if we die will anything happen to you. Driving non-stop, I was taken to Tihar. The media was present here too, furiously clicking pictures of the van. The police had surrounded the Tihar Jail gate. The heavy gates opened, let the car in and I was soon inside. In jail!

32

I was made to strip, then weighed and medically examined. This was the first time I had a proper medical examination. I was asked if I used any intoxicants.

After all the formalities were completed I was taken to the welfare officer. He told me the rules and regulations I had to follow. I learnt that there was a library from where I could borrow books. This made me happy. The deputy jailor soon arrived. He gave me a photograph. It was of some god woman who had a bindi on her forehead. The jailor said, look at this bindi morning and evening, it will bring you peace. He also gave me a thin booklet which contained some spiritual material.

I was then taken to the second gate of the jail. This was just beyond the visitors' room. There was a different kind of police here, the Tamil Nadu Special Police, TSP. There are different kinds of police in the jail for different duties so that they can all keep a check on each other.

The old prisoners, called sevadars, do all the mundane jobs. Once again I was checked thoroughly at this gate. My chappals were also put through the X-ray machine. After this I was taken inside the jail.

The corridors were brightly lit. The walls were graffitied, often with philosophical messages: Hate crime not criminals, said one. It was quite late at night. Prisoners were walking in the barracks and some looked at me curiously. If anyone tried to come close to me, the police pushed him away. Perhaps some of them knew who I was.

I was taken to ward number 4 of jail number 3 – the Mother Teresa ward. I remembered that the first speech I ever gave was about Mother Teresa. I had won a prize, a dictionary. Later, another such speech had made me president of JNU. Now, after yet another speech I was in this jail where I had to live in a ward named after her.

The cell was half the size of my hostel room. It had no windows but had a CCTV attached outside. Both the adjoining cells were empty, giving my small room an even greater air of desolation. There was a western-style commode inside and a small bathing area. A bucket and mug lay on one side and on the other a bedroll with a blanket. Next to it were two bowls – one blue and one red. The colours of our slogan – Jai Bhim Lal Salaam. I smiled at the coincidence.

When you enter politics you know that from that moment on your life will be full of conflicts. Those who you stand against will leave no stone unturned to harm you. I had thought myself prepared but I had never imagined that I would have to go to jail one day. Who was I, after all? Just a young man who was doing research in a university

I knew that I had to ensure that this experience didn't affect me too much. The attack against me was an attack against something larger. The people from my organization, all the students at JNU – everyone was under attack. I had to continue to fight the fight. And to do so, I needed to buffer myself from my surroundings. I could not allow anything to get me down.

This wasn't easy. I had a family which has always had to deal with one problem after another. This could send them over the edge. My mother, father, brother, my thoughts continuously returned home as they had since the day the cop had called my father from the Lodhi Road thana. Would they be safe? With me in jail, would they be targeted too? After 9 February I had started getting anonymous threats against my family. It was hard to feel calm and strong in the middle of such storms.

As always my trick was to reach out to others. Interacting with people had always helped me to overcome my worries and fears; hearing other people's stories distracted me from my own. Since I was on my own in jail, I decided to talk to my solitude.

I sang songs on the first night, a favourite song of the JNU students' movement, 'Dabey pairon se ujala aa raha hai' (The light is creeping in gradually). Any old songs which came to my mind. I sang as heartily as I could, so that the loneliness of the four walls didn't overwhelm me. On the first night I didn't have to try very hard. I was really tired. The attack in the court had left my bones aching. The day itself had drained me emotionally. I had a bath. Since I had no change of clothes I used the sheet to wrap myself. Then covering myself with a blanket, I went off to sleep. I slept soundly.

I woke up in the morning with the arrival of the jailor. He was an intelligent man who was helpful and sympathetic. He asked me about my health and said that people often suffered from depression or anxiety when they first came to jail and that he was worried about me. He asked me to freshen up and then go to his office. He noticed that I did not have any clothes and arranged for a kurta pyjama and a towel. I asked if I could be given the memoirs of Professor Tulsiram, but the jail didn't have a copy and so he got me Premchand's stories and *Nirmala* from the library, and had a TV installed in my cell, like all the other prisoners had.

I was treated as a high-security prisoner with some

special rules. Three men were employed for my security, changing their shifts through the day. A fourth was meant to help me with anything else, get me food, etc. I wasn't allowed out of the cell for meals. My tiny cell became my world.

Lunch was a vegetable, dal, four rotis, onion and salad – carefully based on the calories you were allowed to take. It was the same meal day in, day out. Being a rice eater, I didn't feel full after this meal. The jailor kindly increased the number of rotis.

At night, a guard was placed outside my cell for my security. He was a quiet man. I started talking to him. He was from Tamil Nadu. He loved kabaddi and would lean across the cell door to watch the kabaddi competition playing on the TV in my cell. I always knew the day Tamil Nadu was playing because, when it was time for the match to start, he would ask me hesitantly, are you not watching kabaddi tonight?

The jailor told me that a few political leaders had asked to meet me. I refused. I was allowed to meet ten people whose names I had to write down for him. Not imagining that my family would travel so far to see me, I had filled the list with JNU colleagues and teachers. I said I would only meet those whose names I had written down.

We had begun to develop a cordial relationship and

he went out of his way to make me feel comfortable. He always asked about the people who came to meet me and told me some fascinating things about jail.

For instance, never are only two prisoners kept in a cell because if one were to kill the other, who would be the witness? This is why a cell is usually shared by three or four people. He told me too that in my ward there were two hijras. They had been kept in one cell because there was no other place for them in Tihar.

My first visitors came two days after I had been brought to Tihar. They were two of my lawyer friends. They reassured me that all was well and that I should not worry and put Rs 1000 in my jail card (all prisoners in Tihar are given a card which they can fill with money and use to buy things). I felt much more cheerful after their visit, and was thrilled with their gift. I promptly bought some snacks, feeling relieved that I could eat better.

Slowly the tone of the people in prison began to change. The dry voices became warm. The cold looks dissolved with the change in weather. The policeman outside my cell began to open up to me. He would share his disenchantment with the political state of the country.

He had always wanted to study; he dreamt of doing a PhD. He asked me about JNU – he wanted to know what was so special about it. He was surprised that education was so cheap there. Wistfully, he said his daughter would continue studying, she would do what he hadn't managed to do. I want to get my daughter admitted to JNU, he told me.

33

Even as I began to adapt to prison life, I couldn't help worrying about my jail sentence. How long would I be locked up for? No one seemed to have any answers. To keep the uncertainty away I kept myself busy. It was difficult in an isolated ward with so much security. I was kept away from other prisoners and I was cut off from the activities of the jail. I was taken out for a stroll only when the other cells were shut. Usually I ended up at the multi-religious prayer room, with its pictures of Shirdi Sai Baba and Subhas Chandra Bose, just walking around the empty hall.

I started exercising to keep myself busy. I would jump and try to touch the high ceiling in my room although I never succeeded. I tried to build a relationship with my space. I started to sweep the floor diligently. Even if I saw a speck of dust I would clean it up. I washed my plate with care. I counted the iron bars; I tried to measure the length and breadth of my cell.

I now ate my food slowly, tasting every bite. As a poor student and student activist I never really gave food too much thought. I simply thought of filling my stomach. Now I began to pay attention to what I was eating – even though the food was not very good.

A whitish pigeon would come into my cell through the exhaust fan vent. I spent a lot of time looking at it. The singing continued. I would also talk to myself. The college debater got a second life in that quiet cell. I would speak for and against the motion – a good way to test my argument.

I tried to keep my mind away from what was happening in the outside world and not think of things which made me feel isolated, disheartened and lonely. I read the newspapers and watched the news only briefly. The moment I read or saw anything on JNU my mind would be assailed with memories and I would feel unsettled. I started watching other entertainment programme – films and sports – as a way to distract myself.

My efforts paid off. I began to feel calmer. Things improved further when I began to keep a diary. I knew that I would find it difficult to capture my feelings in words. It's like trying to define the sweetness of two different fruits. But I forced myself to begin, thinking it was important to record these experiences.

I mostly stayed in my cell. If there were any visitors I went to meet them and then returned to the cell. Once in a while I spoke with some inmates. My fellow inmates were a varied lot. There were people who had been there for years with no one to bail them out. There were some who came from good backgrounds. Many suffered from psychological ailments.

A community radio played during the day. The radio jockey was a Bihari. He was convicted in a murder case. He was educated and sensible. He'd come and ask me which song to play and played songs of my choice – *'Zindagi tu hi bata irada kya hai'*. Apart from the sevadar who I became very close to, I spoke mostly to him.

I ended up having some interesting chats with a few others. There was a man who had once been a Rajya Sabha MP. He was quite advanced in years and could not possibly attack anyone. So when I came out of my cell he was not locked up. One day he said to me, 'This BJP government is fraud.' I wanted to know what he meant by this.

He told me that the government had jailed him for having built a temple. 'I have built a temple in Delhi,' he said. 'Whenever there is a BJP government I am locked up because they say I have made money in building the temple. This government is into temple politics. On the promise that Ram Mandir will be made who knows how much money has been collected from common people? Where have the bricks gone? Where is the donation money? And I'm the one who is repeatedly thrown into jail.'

There was another prisoner who happened to be a very rich businessman. One day he said to me that in this country, businessmen are not respected. He was involved in a scam.

He asked me, 'Now you tell me, can any business flourish without a scam? Politicians themselves do it. But the scam that a businessman does is not a scam – it is business.'

I said, 'Sir, people have turned politics into business.'

He said, 'You're right. These days it's hard to tell the difference between politics and business.'

34

One day my brother and chacha came to visit me. It was a complete surprise. I hadn't expected them to make such a long journey. What surprised me even more was that others from my village had also come to see me. Both reassured me and asked me not to worry.

I was feeling strong but after meeting them I felt stronger still. Before they left, they gave me Ma's number. That evening, hearing her voice on the phone filled me with emotion. My parents had been on my mind so much. Ma as usual was very strong. It's okay, she said, you've done nothing wrong. My family doesn't make me weak – it makes me strong.

I had other visitors too which relieved the monotony of the days. One day a group of lawyers, whom I didn't know, sent a bail petition to be signed. I sent it back. They sent it again. They were voluntarily coming to fight my case. A lot of teachers, activists and leading figures from the CPI came to meet me. Everyone raised my morale but they also reminded me how harsh prison is. There is so much we have to give up when we go in – talking to people we are close to is one of them. The things you take for granted are often the greatest of luxuries.

One day, the jailor told me, a distant cousin had come to see me. She waited a whole day and had to leave because her name was not on my visitors' list. I realized how little I thought of my family, how little I am conscious of my duty towards them.

One realizes the importance of the biggest and smallest things in jail. Family, companionship, conversation. But also of small things like a nail cutter. I had to wait for two days to get one and take special permission since it can be used as a weapon. For the same reason, the looking glass is made of fibre and there are no metallic nails in the cell.

One day I asked for a shave. The barber was called. Five people surrounded me as I was shaved – three staff members, one ward-in-charge and the person who had brought the barber. They were there for my protection and also to make sure that I didn't snatch the barber's instruments and hurt anyone. I was both dangerous and in danger myself.

Life in jail is based on suspicion and lack of faith in each other. Though this is usually not so obvious, it becomes apparent in some situations. For instance, when the doctor comes to inspect your food, you can feel the paranoia in the air. He has to taste the food. If the food is poisoned the doctor will die first. Such lack of faith! The doctor looks at the sevadar. The sevadar looks at the doctor. Then the doctor takes a bite, gives me my food and walks away.

35

I had been in jail for about a week now when once again I was sent to police remand. The judge came to the jail for the hearing. This time the police was doing a joint questioning along with Umar and Anirban who were involved in the 9 February programme.

I had seen news of Umar's and Anirban's surrender on TV. After my arrest, the students who had organized the programme had gone into hiding and later two of them had given themselves up. I was a little apprehensive about Umar, as a lot of cops had been quoted as saying they'd bash him up if they caught him.

The three of us were made to sit together. We were meeting each other for the first time in nearly two weeks. I was delighted to see my old colleagues. In JNU we belonged to different political groups, and would often criticize and attack each other. But we had been bound together by this attack.

All three of us asked each other the same question – had we been beaten while we were in custody? I was relieved to hear that, like me, they too had been treated well.

There wasn't much questioning. It was just a formality. For instance, they asked Umar, do you know Kanhaiya? He said, yes.

Kanhaiya, do you know Umar?

Yes, I do.

How do you know him?

Both of us replied, we live on the same campus.

Any political connection?

Umar said we had no political connection. We belonged to different organizations.

Did Kanhaiya help you in the 9 February programme?

Umar said there was no need for help, a poster could be printed for Rs 150.

When permission was cancelled for your function that day, did you call Kanhaiya?

Umar said, yes, I did, but his phone was switched off.

The next question too was to Umar: how was your function held without Kanhaiya's permission?

Umar said, Kanhaiya is the JNUSU president, not the president of the USA.

Once the questioning was over, Umar and Anirban were sent back and I returned to my cell.

They said that they too would be following me to jail but I could see that we were nearing the end of the road. As we parted, I saw a day when each of us would be free and return to our beloved JNU. I felt light for the first time in weeks.

36

It was 2 March. I remained opposed to applying for bail and insisted that all charges against all students be dropped. But the AISF, after consulting lawyers, decided to file a bail application. The bail petition was to be heard any day now. I hadn't switched on the TV that day. I knew all kinds of nonsensical discussions would be going on. There was no point listening to them. All said, I was sick of the news channels. I knew my truth – how could I bear to see all the lies being spread about me?

I got the news of my bail plea being accepted from the same TSP constable who watched kabaddi with me. He told me that I would be quietly eased out of jail any day now. The paperwork had taken some time so they couldn't let me go that day.

I asked if I'd be allowed to go next morning. I was told that convicts are not released in the daytime. It would be after five in the evening.

I was to spend one more day in prison.

3 March.

My last day here. Many convicts came to meet me. The radio jockey said if he could escape, he'd come to meet me. After this I went to meet the jailor, who had asked to see me. On my way out, I saw the sevadar cleaning the adjoining cell. He told me he was preparing the cell for a new occupant.

The jailor confirmed that I'd be released that evening. He asked me where I'd like to go. Home?

I said, 'Yes, I'd like to go home. JNU is my home.'

He asked where I'd stay.

My hostel, I replied.

I learnt that the two new occupants in my ward were to be Umar and Anirban. I later discovered that Anirban was put in my cell, Umar in the one adjoining.

On returning from the jailor's office, I called the sevadar and gave him my clothes and towel – since I wasn't allowed to leave with any possessions. He had been in jail for ten years now under Section 307. He had really taken good care of me and I felt very close to him. I wanted to give him something more. But what could I give him? I remembered that my friend had put Rs 1000 in my jail card. I hadn't spent most of it. I gave him that card.

I left the jail on a bike in the same clothes I had walked

in in two weeks earlier. My lawyer friends and some teachers had come to meet me. Because there was a crowd outside the gate and the police didn't want a scene, I was put on a bike and made to leave through the residential area in the back. A police van was parked at a distance. I was made to get into it and we drove off, away from Tihar Jail, away from the last twenty days. Twenty days which had seemed to me like a lifetime.

We entered JNU from the western gate and I was dropped off at Professor Ajay Patnaik's residence. There was a huge crowd waiting for me. People were falling over each other trying to take pictures. I had been away from JNU for twenty days. Dazed, numbed by the crowds, I found myself feeling distanced from it. JNU meant your dhaba, your hostel, your room – but they all felt far away. So much had come in the way.

I was surrounded and taken to the open space behind the administrative block which has been lovingly renamed Azadi Chowk by teachers and students after my arrest. When we got there I saw a large gathering. Seeing them, I forgot all my uncertainties, my disorientation. I was with my people.

The people who knew me, those who had elected me and whose trust I had to keep. The people who had fought for me. Those who had filled twenty-one buses to march on the roads of Delhi seeking my release. These were my people. My comrades, my teachers, staff – all of whom had made my struggle possible. Who had taught me that the biggest battles in the world can be fought and won together.

Now I had to speak in front of them. But they were not the only ones in the audience. As I saw the rows of cameras lined up in the back, I realized that in my audience were the millions of people of this country. I had to address the nation from this Azadi Chowk.

As always, I had no prepared speech to give. Whatever I had seen in the last few weeks, whatever I had experienced, the conversations I had had in prison with inmates and police – these were the things I now needed to present as my first address to the nation.

I talked about the attacks against me and the university and the reasons behind these attacks. It was said that JNU students lived on subsidies and made anti-national speeches. A sort of binary was being created in the press between anti-national JNU students and the patriotic soldiers who had recently died in a tragic accident in Siachen.

I had to reply to this attack. I also had to expose the Sangh Parivar and the false propagandists of the government. But mere attack was not going to be enough. I also had to give my audience what I thought was a solution.

The students who had raised questions were accused of biting the hands which fed us. Those who take crores and misuse that money – what do they do? This was the question I had to pose.

Why was the integrity of poor students, dependent on subsidy, doubted? Why weren't questions asked of the leaders who embezzled crores and acted innocent? How had political parties who had worked against the country been given the moral right to question our nationalism?

Why were only the poor expected to give evidence of their integrity? How could those who betrayed the nation issue certificates of nationalism?

It was not just a speech, it was a conversation about rights, powers and the future of the young in this country. It was a conversation that had begun earlier, and for which I had been arrested. Now I was to start that conversation again.

I walked towards the mike. I could see the faces in front of me, the challenges that lay ahead.

Epilogue

I've begun a new life. The young boy who once hesitated to stand in the front row during protest demonstrations has suddenly come under the spotlight of national and world media. I have no private life left. I am always surrounded by people, security guards and media.

After I came out of prison, I received hundreds of letters – some carried warm love and support, while others were full of abuse and hatred. I felt that I had been shifted from a small jail to a big, open prison. But then I realized that for the people who had come out into the streets, who had been beaten up and abused, who constantly faced police cases and other forms of oppression, for them too this world is an open jail. They are also bound by the chains of casteism, patriarchy, inequality. There should be a fight to bring down this wall of exploitation, to transform this world from an open jail to a place where free thinking people can live and where equality, justice and humanity can reign on.

But I have to admit that even as this new turn in my life made me more politically determined, it didn't always personally make me happy. What I said now became news, I wasn't used to this and it made me uncomfortable. It was also very troubling. I seemed to have lost my ease and freedom. I could no longer meet my fellow students in the campus nor could I sit in the dhabas and talk to them freely at any time. I couldn't even live in my hostel room by myself. I am energized meeting people. I love talking about politics and current issues, I love moving around freely interacting with strangers, exchanging ideas with them. Now I couldn't do any of this. My relationship with my friends too had changed.

Journalists were always waiting for me to say something, to meet me. I sometimes liked this because the media could help me reach out to the people directly. But I have also come to realize that the press are looking for something more than my ideas – something which could create a controversy.

I finally went home after four months of being released to address a public meeting in Begusarai. My home was also not the home of the past. There was a large number of people who came to meet me. I had a big contingent of security guards and if I had stayed at home they couldn't have been accommodated. So I had to sleep at a neighbour's house so that they could be on my security.

The principal of Sunrise Public School, Ramkumarji, met me and overcome by emotion started crying. He gave me laddoos and mangoes. He said, 'A teacher's life is fulfilled when the student he has taught becomes famous. I feel that my life has been a success.'

I tried to remember the child who used to be scolded by his mother for dirtying his school uniform, for whose education milk had been stopped at home, who tried very hard to adjust to the new culture of a public school. But the dust of the fleeting days has covered those feelings. Returning home made me realize how far I left those memories behind.

~

After coming out of the jail I decided to go to Hyderabad. The Hyderabad of Rohith Vemula – after all we were fighting for justice for him when I was arrested. Then began a tour around the country. From Nagpur, the headquarters of RSS, against which Hyderabad began its fight, to the progressive villages of Kerala. From the massive rallies in Mumbai to rallies of freedom in Una, slowly this fight was taking the shape of an all-India movement.

Wherever I went, people came to meet me every day. Students, government employees, corporate employees, youth, artists, people who were sick of the system and who felt that the existing system was an enemy of humanity and prosperity. They all wanted to be part of each other's problems and the struggle against them.

On my return from Pune to Delhi on an Air India flight, even the captain came out to receive me. Once everyone had left the craft, he took me to a corner seat of the plane. Then he called the other crew members. Each of them started telling me about their problems.

Some farmers came to meet me in Gujarat whose land had been taken away by the Adani Group for its power plant. Once an Indian Muslim woman from Saudi Arabia stopped me in Mumbai and told me, 'You are Kanhaiya, aren't you...I wanted to tell you something. Keep our country safe.'

Before going to jail I had never imagined that I would one day go to jail. Before becoming the president of JNUSU I had never imagined that I could win. I had never imagined becoming a student of JNU before getting admission here. While living in Mukherjee Nagar I had dreams of becoming a civil servant, a district magistrate perhaps; today people ask me if I want to contest elections.

I cannot say how the tide will turn. But no matter what comes in the future, I have decided my role; I want to fight for all those people who tell me their stories, for a better society for the next generation.

~

On my last day in prison the jail security guard told me a story about a prince who wins the hand of the princess in marriage and the reins of the kingdom. But having achieved victory, the prince builds a throne so high for himself that it has to be climbed by a staircase.

The guard wanted to know why the prince did this.

This wasn't just his question. It is a question the majority of the people of the country are asking. Why does the prime minister who came on the promise of better days or achhe din wear a nine-lakh-rupee suit, while weavers are committing suicide due to debts? Why when he has to worry about the price of lentils and tomatoes is he modelling for private companies?

People want to know why the ruler of the country has built his throne in the sky. They feel cheated. They are raising questions on the foundation of this throne.

We only have one way ahead. Babasaheb has said that we have to get educated or we will not understand the problems facing our society. Nor can we fight these problems single-handedly. For this we will have to be organized. But just being organized won't help unless we decide to agitate. The problems we are facing demand a united fight.

The people united shall always be victorious.

Acknowledgements

A person's life is not just his own – the contributions of his family and the society play a large part in it. And the way the toiling masses of this country have expressed their love and support, it always gives me strength and affirmation. In this are included my friends, teachers, comrades of JNUSU, friends of all organizations, staff and security guards of JNU and comrades of my own organization, the AISF, and the JNU community. I will always be grateful to you.

Idris is the first one who told me to write a book. Thank you.

Aakansha, Chandrika and Amrita, thank you for helping me write this book. Gopal and Gavin Morris, for the cover you made.

Reyazul Haque, who spent nights and days working on this book and gave it shape.

Acknowledgements

Chiki Sarkar and Renu Agal at Juggernaut, who worked till the last day to make it a better read.

As this book is now among readers, thanks to Varun and Nishant who managed my time and kept me in touch during my journeys and busy schedule.

A Note on the Author

Kanhaiya Kumar, an AISF activist, was the president of the JNU Students' Union 2015–16. He is pursuing his PhD from the Centre for African Studies at the School of International Studies, JNU, New Delhi.

1

CRAFTED
FOR MOBILE
READING

*Thought you would never read a book
on mobile? Let us prove you wrong.*

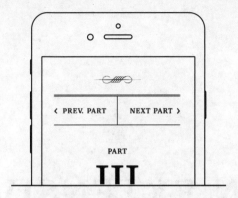

Beautiful Typography

The quality of print transferred
to your mobile. Forget ugly PDFs.

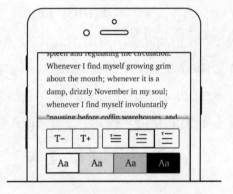

Customizable Reading

Read in the font size, spacing
and background of your liking.

AN EXTENSIVE LIBRARY

Including fresh, new, original Juggernaut books from the likes of Sunny Leone, Praveen Swami, Husain Haqqani, Umera Ahmed, Rujuta Diwekar and lots more. Plus, books from partner publishers and loads of free classics. Whichever genre you like, there's a book waiting for you.

DON'T JUST READ; INTERACT

We're changing the reading experience from passive to active.

Ask authors questions

Get all your answers from the horse's mouth.
Juggernaut authors actually reply to every
question they can.

Rate and review

Let everyone know of your favourite reads or
critique the finer points of a book – you will be
heard in a community of like-minded readers.

Gift books to friends

For a book-lover, there's no nicer gift than
a book personally picked. You can even
do it anonymously if you like.

Enjoy new book formats

Discover serials released in parts over
time, picture books including comics,
and story-bundles at discounted rates.
And coming soon, audiobooks.

4

LOWEST PRICES & ONE-TAP BUYING

Books start at ₹10 with regular discounts and free previews.

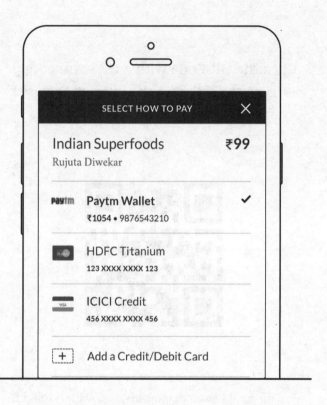

Paytm Wallet, Cards & Apple Payments

On Android, just add a Paytm Wallet once and buy any book with one tap. On iOS, pay with one tap with your iTunes-linked debit/credit card.

Click the QR Code with a QR scanner app
or type the link into the Internet browser
on your phone to download the app.

For our complete catalogue, visit www.juggernaut.in
To submit your book, send a synopsis and two
sample chapters to books@juggernaut.in
For all other queries, write to contact@juggernaut.in